Blending Cultures

Blending Cultures

A guide for ESL Teachers and students

JOHN D. TRUBON

iUniverse, Inc.
Bloomington

Blending Cultures
A guide for ESL Teachers and students

iUniverse books may be ordered through booksellers or by contacting:

iUniverse
1663 Liberty Drive
Bloomington, IN 47403
www.iuniverse.com
1-800-Authors (1-800-288-4677)

ISBN: 978-1-4620-4247-0 (sc)
ISBN: 978-1-4620-4248-7 (ebk)

Printed in the United States of America

iUniverse rev. date: 09/23/2011

CONTENTS

Foreward

Teaching English as a second language or as a foreign language is an exciting challenge. There are so many factors that influence the work the teachers do. One thing is for sure, niether the teacher or student will ever be the same after the classes are over.

The teacher will have a much broader perspective on the world and feel much more comfortable in a foreign, cultural environment. The student will also have an expanded. mind and most likely increased abilities in what are unrelated fields. The brain will be changed and both the left and right sides will function better.

Much research has been done to determine the relationships between culture and language. There has also been lots of research that has determined that language actually shapes the way people think!!! Attitudes are very different when one speaks more than one language with the language being used influencing the feelings and attitudes of the speaker. For example, when an Arabian person speaks Arabic when talking about a Jewish person their attitude and feelings are very different than when they speak about the same person while speaking Hebrew.

When one is involved in the language teaching profession it soon becomes apparent that the thinking patterns of the students are quite different in the various countries the teacher can find themselves working in. The question then arises, does the Language shape the thinking or is it the culture that shapes the thinking because language is an expression of the culture. The ultimate outcome is that regardless of what shapes what there is a very definite need to be sensitive to these influences and take them into consideration as one helps the students acquire a new language and use it proficiently. This can only happen if there is a connection coupled with cultural sensitivity on the part of the teacher. There is definite proof that there is a definite increase in other abilities demonstrated by bi-lingual people. The arts and musical abilities are very much heightened as one example.

Introduction

There are strong and increasing pressures in most societies now in these times of surging economic changes. Financial hardship is common for some retirees as well as high unemployment for many of the younger people. The world is changing rapidly and English is ever becoming the dominant language of commerce. Growing numbers of the older generations still feel active and in need of something to do with their lives as things are changing.

Many people read the advertisments for volunteers or for the schools and colleges that offer language teacher training to enable English Language Teachers to work abroad. They, quite naturally, think it would be a nice way to travel economically and see some other parts of the world, at little or no expense, while they still have the time and energy.

I was one of these people although I was not really retired at that time, just freshly Divorced and bored with living alone in an apartment instead of a house in the country.
I was fortunate in as much that I had already travelled quite extensively. I chose to try to teach Business English to company executives because in my quite extensive business travelling. I had come to realize the big differences in the usage of the English language one encountered in the various countries. This had caught my attention as I had been an executive myself in an international corporation in London England for some years previously. I was aware that these language differences could possibly and often did lead to big misunderstandings and large, immediate financial losses as well as the future loss of potential business. The problems were not just poor use of langauge but largely due to lack of comprehension because of the cultural differences and erroneously understanding of words that had been directly translated using a Dictionary.

I had experience in teaching technical subjects when I was younger so I took an English Second Language Teacher training Course and set out to see more of the world.

Having already thought quite a lot about the possible causes of the language usage
 differences and had arrived at some conclusions but still totally unaware of the size of the problems which face many English teachers. Now, with more than thirteen years of English second language teaching experience I feel that I have finally found many of the answers.

The ESL Teacher training courses do not prepare you for the difficulties that can be experienced in the field as a result of cultural unawareness and even more from the tremendous effect culture has on language as well as language acquisition. In many countries you will encounter people from many of the English speaking countries working temporarily in the language schools and trying to teach their language to the local people. They have been hired on the assumption that a native speaker can easily teach their mother tongue. The schools have realized that their own, home grown, teachers have some difficulties with pronunciation and lack of the ability to be able to explain the nuances and idiosyncrasies of the English language and think that a native speaker can easily rectify that. They do not realize that although the native speakers can speak their own language and communicate with their fellow countrymen quite well they have never had to study in depth the reasons for the idiosyncrasies. The native speakers can speak their local kind of English from wherever they came from but they do not use middle of the road, internationally understood English. The students in another country find the native speakers difficult to understand. The English language varies from place to place, quite a lot, due to local socioeconomic conditions, education level, life style and things that influence their understanding. These Tourist style teachers have no clear cut understanding of the way that their culture affects the teacher and the students.

This small book is written to try to help overcome some of these difficulties, improve the lot of the teacher and the quality of the language their students learn to speak.

Chapter one

When you have acquired your English Teacher's Certificate you will be all fired up and ready to go. Then you learn that the world of the language teacher is not what you expected it to be or what you were led to believe. Firstly, you find that you are not a special kind of person you are only ordinary. You are only one of many visitors going to work to make money for a new employer in a foreign country and environment. Many of the school owners think they are doing the new teacher a big favour by allowing them to work in their school on a Tourist Visa. You will soon realize that you are employed to just do a job and do it well by using the teaching materials provided by the employer regardless of the quality of the material given you to use. Many of the language schools are a franchise and as such they have to use the course material that is provided by the franchise holder and the quality as well as the teaching method is questionable in many cases.

When you go out into the Language School world you will find that there are many course books available and they have been written by all kinds of people such as university professors in various institutions around the world down to not very well educated but experienced Language Teachers, who have been working in the field and think they have a better way to teach. They all have something to offer but the do not help the teacher or the reader understand why that particular book has some advantages over the others. This is because more explanation and understanding is needed and a changed approach by the authors and the teacher. Some of the Course Books have been written by teachers in the country you find yourself in and they have the same problems as the teachers from that country. The success for the student is usually left entirely in the hands of the teacher and how they handle the course material.

One of the first things a new teacher notices is that most students need to have the material being taught offered to them in a different manner for each individual because they are in reality, all, very much, individuals. They nearly all learn in a different ways. Some are aurally orientated, others are visually stimulated while others need to see or experience what it is they are trying to learn, hands on, many of them need a mixture of these ways. Students are all different, coming from different environments and they certainly are not like little pots, sitting in their desks that you stand in front of, and fill with your linguistic knowledge.

In the beginning most of us remember and often emulate the teachers we had when we were young and in the lower grades in school. The teachers were rather authoritarian in their approach to us their students. They would take out their teacher's books or notes and start to talk or write on the board with their squeaky chalk stick and you would then copy what they said or wrote. The information they passed on to you was supposed to be absorbed and understood. Those teachers took the credit for our success but most of the understanding came from our interaction with our peers and family.

If a person went to classes to learn another language and in many schools this was not an option but compulsory, they would usually be put in a big class and learn mostly the grammar and vocabulary of the target language and how to read that language by remembering 'word lists' and grammar lists. You did not learn how to communicate with another person by talking to them. There was little or no interaction between the students or the teacher. This is called the 'Grammar translation method', it serves no really useful purpose unless the student just wants to read and understand a book that is written in whatever foreign language they hope to learn. There is no hope of having an interactive lesson with a large class but there is no other option and it is only possible to use this method when the classes are large, more than eight students is a rough guide so it is advisable to limit class size,

Nowadays things are very different, the students learn 'whole language' and they do so by interacting a lot with the other students and the teacher. Yet, there are still great barriers that slow down the process. The main barrier to language learning is the difference in the cultures of the two countries; the country of the student and the target language. The cultural difference also presents problems for the foreign teacher when working in another country. The teacher is initially unaware of the differences but must be sensitive to the local people and their culture. The students who are immersed in their own native culture find it difficult to grasp the concepts and the real meaning of the words in the new language and there are several reasons why this is so.

Culture starts to be assimilated immediately we are born. We learn how to act and react from our experiences with other people. Our culture has developed in our society and the society of others over centuries. It is influenced by the physical environment where we live as well as the cultural and societal as well as the family environment. We learn how to behave and react to the stimulation of the others, to understand and be socially acceptable to them. The difficulties start to become apparent when the others react differently to what we expect. The very structural integrity, coherency and stability of our personalities are rooted in our culture and we act and react accordingly.

We can research culture on the internet and find that there has been lots of research done on the subject because in these days of rapid and easy international travel, many people find themselves experiencing Culture Clash or even the more severe Culture Shock and feeling very confused and uncomfortable when in a new, strange environment.

If we should take a closer look at the subject and get a handle on what we, as teachers, are dealing with. It really helps us as teachers if we can understand the dynamics of what is happening in our classrooms.

Many people have problems adjusting to living in a different cultural environment because it is an all pervading influence on our personal experiences. In fact culture is a Mind Set. The Latin countries have very different cultures to Europe or North America while the Asian countries are yet another story. Eastern Europe and the Slavic countries and what were parts of the Communist bloc are yet another experience. This gives rise to many difficulties for people visiting these places until they adjust their thinking and accept the fact that the local people will not change their ways in their own country and the visitor must adapt, accept the new culture, go with the flow and change their mind set to fit in.

Every culture is different because it developed to enable the local residents to relate to one another in their environment at their location as it attempts to create a universal discourse for its members. This is the way with which people can interpret and understand their experiences and convey them to one another. Without a common system of codifying sensations and experiences, life would be ridiculous or even absurd and all efforts to share meaning would be doomed to failure. It's accepted that culture powerfully influences thoughts, emotions and behaviors. In fact, culture operates in our primary cognitive, perceptual and motivational levels.

Culture is an important part of our blueprint for operation within our physical and social worlds. We, as humans, are an insecure species and culture offers us a reduction of anxiety through its standard rules of thought, emotion and behavior.
Culture offers us the security that comes from predictability in an often unpredictable world. We see things through a cultural filter that tints, magnifies, shrinks and otherwise shapes our perceptions.

Our culture is a mindset that we developed during childhood. The structural integrity, coherency and stability of our personalities and language are rooted in our culture. It is for these and other reasons that intercultural interactions can cause anxiety and often strongly stimulate our negative emotions.

When people of different cultures meet there can be uncertainty and confusion about the rules of the interaction. Many of our basic assumptions do not fit the situation. Our normally successful thoughts, emotions and behaviors do not get the responses and give the feedback we are accustomed to. Some of our expectations regarding the outcome and meaning of social interactions are not confirmed. When we are in a social interaction situation in another culture we may think, feel or behave in the manner we are normally accustomed to in such a situation and then find that it just doesn't work. We expect to be understood and we expect a certain response from other people, but we either get no response at all or we get a response that is completely different from what we expect. We might even be so misunderstood that we cause hurt feelings, anger or resentment, or we feel these ourselves. And even if we don't experience these strong emotions, we frequently feel confused.

The purpose for which the student is learning another language rather influences the way they and the teacher approached the lessons. This is what Mz Hoffman was talking about, in her book, Lost in translation, when she wrote, "*English is not the language of my Soul.*" To understand this we have to take a look at the differences in the value systems in the different societies in the countries that we might be teaching in. For example, if we look at the values of the Inuit or Eskimo of just a relatively short time ago who lived in Igloos built out of snow, they had no furniture and even their language had no word for 'sit' because they relaxed and slept on animal skins on the floor. The Igloos were not very warm out of necessity because if they got too warm inside they would melt and leave the occupants exposed to the elements. The Eskimo man would loan his wife to any visitors who stayed over night so that she could keep them warm. This is not practiced in our society and there certainly is not much of that going on in our cities, in fact I would be rather frowned upon. The meaning or value of the word fidelity, for example, is rather different for the Inuit.

The British history of tolerating the Puritans and their attitude towards physical contact between any of the people, even when playing sports, and seeing it as contrary to their religious beliefs rather put a different value on expressions of affection between the different sexes. Queen Victoria really put the finishing touches to that situation while she reigned. Her attitude of, "I am not amused" towards anything she thought to be vulgar coupled with her intolerance towards public demonstrations of affection This led to the miserable years of the Victorian era where marriage and wives were just for procreation and mistresses were for sexual entertainment and pleasure for the men. Many of Queen Victoria's values still pervade the societies in the countries that were part of the now extinct British Empire or the colonies.

Anyone who visited the Communist bloc of countries can also appreciate the difference in the meaning of the word honesty between those countries and ours. The Communist ideals of equality were rather contrary to human nature and being as all the people were paid equally the only way to have more that your neighbour was to steal what someone else had. One of the legacies of Communism is dishonesty, corruption and thieving.

The Latino countries have very different moral values as well as attitudes towards the sanctity of marriage when you compare them to those in England and many others of the developed, 'First World' countries. Their attitude towards time is also very different. We from the First World find their attitude of 'maybe we'll do it tomorrow' when it comes to responding to another persons needs to be rather irritating when we try to do business with them. As an example, their not confirming receipt of our business enquiries leads us to look elsewhere for what we want to purchase because we have no idea if they received our enquiry or if we will ever hear from them.
The Latino way of greeting friends and relative with hugs and kisses and touching each other when engaged in conversation is very much in contrast with the North American need for their rather large personal body zones. The value placed on intimacy is greatly contrasted under those circumstances. I personally had difficulty in adjusting to living in France where it is the norm to greet both male and female friends by kissing them on both cheeks. It was even more difficult to fit in when one met a male friend in the early morning when he was on the way home after a night of drinking and carousing. I did not like the rough, stubbly face with the odor of stale beer, tobacco smoke and Garlic mixed with the perfume of his catch of the day before. Trying to fit in with Canadians after Paris took quite some time.

In the Third World countries where large families are the norm and the families living all together in crowded conditions so they can all contribute to the family's income, personal property rights as well as privacy hardly exist. The Muslim attitude towards polygamy, women's dress and the way they are very restricted in their relationships with men. The stoning to death for adultery and honour killing is regarded as more than severe by the other cultures. Society's attitude in the countries where polygamy is acceptable and the East Indian acceptance of the Khama Sutra and the Tantric religion certainly put a different perspective on family life.

I believe that you can now start to appreciate the problems that arise with teaching language when words have very different values and even meanings when translated from one language to another. The examples are numerous but I think you can grasp the need for great consideration when trying to teach students how to understand the other person and their reactions when they meet a native speaker.

Chapter two

When we are born we had no ability to speak with our mother or the other members of the family. We very quickly learned how to communicate by making sounds and actions. Mother interprets these and understands or guesses what it is needed. As we grow a little older we have been listening a lot to the way the older people around us communicate by talking and using facial expressions as well as gestures and we start to connect the sounds they make and the reactions they get in return. We then start to use one or two words at a time to get our needs met more efficiently. If we are lucky and choose the right words, it works. We have little else to do at that time except eat, sleep and try to get whatever else it is we need to be comfortable while we grow.

It seems like a small miracle that by the time we are about two years of age we have quite a good grasp of the language with a quite extensive vocabulary. We are fortunate that mentally we are a clean slate and do not have anything else to keep our minds occupied or any preconceptions to get in the way of our language acquisition.

When we are older we find ourselves busy with our lives and no longer have the openness of the small child because we have been conditioned by society and have adopted their culture, and their value system as well as moral codes and ethical standards. We have also become self conscious and feel very uncomfortable when we are compelled to try to use another language. It can be really crushing for an adult or teenager who has a good command of their own language to find themselves reduced to the verbal communication skills of a young toddler when trying to use the target language.
If you are on a business trip or even just on holiday you find that there are severe limits on your social life as well as any other activities you might wish to pursue. The Mr. Macho man really feels the pinch under these circumstances.

One can only wonder why these difficulties exist when we had no problem learning a language when we were just a baby. This is where it starts to get interesting for the serious language teacher. The problems arise because our language is an expression of us and the understanding we have of the other people, when we talk to them with a translation of our language, the message they get is often quite different to the message we are trying to convey. We try to communicate and convey concepts but the understanding just is not there.

There have been many studies carried out on language acquisition but most of them concentrated on the time when the subjects were children. As an adult the situation is vastly different. The adult language student has already mastered a language, developed a social network as well as a lot of self esteem and expectations together with social skills. They find the reduction in their ability to communicate to be quite a shock because it presents them with many difficulties.

Using the Telephone is another, really big challenge for anyone trying to use that device when using a second language. Research has determined that when we use the Telephone, we lose 93% of our ability to communicate. There is no longer any help from gestures, facial expressions, body language, or any other way that two people communicate when face to face. We are strictly limited to our understanding of the words used.

One of the first things the teacher will become aware of is the limited understanding they actually have of their own language. Teaching another language makes this lack of understanding quite apparent. Being asked questions by a student from another country can be a real 'eye opener'. The native speaker just learned the language by mainly Osmosis it just soaked in when they weren't looking, just busy living, talking and listening. Now we find that our students need to have good explanations and, "That's just the way it is said" is not good enough. We have to know why and be able to cite rules or reasons. We find ourselves really searching for this understanding and just reading Grammar books does not do the trick. Because we grew up and were educated in our native tongue we needed little in the way of explanation in our English classes at school when most of our problems were quite small and mostly just simple spelling errors or grammatical in nature.

Pronunciation is another big challenge. When trying to teach pronunciation the teacher will most likely find that the students forget the different sounds of the letters and so they pronounce words with their native language letter sounds and it is difficult for them to change. Because of this they do not recognize the words when they hear them spoken by a native speaker.

Teaching English has extra challenges in this regard because English is a stressed timed, rhythmic language unlike French, Spanish, German, Italian and many other syllabic languages. The pronunciation is adjusted to maintain the rhythm of English in many ways and the extra levels of stress and unstress of some of the syllables is difficult for the students to grasp.

For people who would like to get an insight into the way language shapes a great part of our lives I recommend that you take a look a how others have coped. There is a good book written by a woman PhD called Eva Hoffman who was not a native English speaker which throws a lot of light on this subject. The book is Entitled, "Lost in Translation" The authoress was a young girl in Poland and she, with her family, escaped the Russian occupation and went to Canada when she was just twelve years old. She and her sister learned English on the streets of Vancouver while going to school even though they could not speak English when they arrived.

The authoress was quite brilliant and was awarded scholarships. She went to several universities the final one of them being Harvard where she qualified for her PhD in English Literature. The woman became the literary critic for the New York Times. She was married and divorced twice and in the book she quite graphically explains the difficulties she had in her life because English was not her native tongue or as she says in one place in the book, "The language of my Soul". She said she had no problem writing the university papers because, for her, words were just things and things can be manipulated but communicating directly and completely with others is a very different thing.

Why would this woman have these experiences when she is so obviously skilled in the English language, the reasons are based in her culture with its unique set of cultural values? She was Polish and Jewish with very a different background, value system, ethical values as well as morality which were passed on to her by her parents and the society she grew up in. She lived by these values while those around her lived by their own cultural standards and expectations. It was a very long time before she could say, "I am finally living in English". This took her a long time because our language is linked to our culture and emotions so we express ourselves as we think we are.

When we try to teach others how to speak our language we start to notice that a word can mean something different, even to another native speaker depending upon their life experiences. For example, take a simple word, like Mother or Father. If the person grew up in a home with an attentive, loving, caring mother the image that comes to mind and the feelings when they hear that word will be warm and welcome. The understanding will be considerably different than if they grew up with a non caring self centred mother who neglected them or even abused them. The same thing applies to many other words such as happiness, pleasure love, home and so on, the number is great.

This may not seem applicable at first but if you think about it, Culture is not just confined to nations or classifications of large groups of peoples like European, Latino or Oriental. There are national characteristics and cultural trends but within that population you will find variations as you travel to different areas of that country. They use their language differently with local slang expressions. They have local dialects that can be confusing to a stranger. Then if you look at the families within your own community you will again notice that each family has different values as well as different senses of morality and ethics. We now start to realize that all of the different communities are made up of a multitude of micro cultures that all have different understandings. This situation also exists in other countries.

Life is a subjective experience for us all and we make and understand our own, self created reality. This is what makes getting married an interesting exercise. When two people are dating but living at home with their family, they have little problem with accepting the other person but when they start to live together, full time, on a daily basis the differences in understanding and values become apparent and often irritating for both of them. The situation is often aggravated by the couple having different methods of coping with this irritation. Both of them want to overcome the hurdle that now exists but the both have great difficulty modifying their reactions to the stressful stimulation. Abraham Maslow wrote lots of things on this subject. It is very hard for anyone to behave contrary to their cultural background and expectations. At one time when I attended at twenty five years of marriage celebration I head the Priest who had conducted the original marriage ceremony say. "When they came to the Church I thought, as I looked at them, I know that love is blind but marriage will restore their vision."

Their have been many studies carried out on language acquisition but most of them were trying to determine how a child learned to talk. There have also been many studies carried out on culture, the effect on language learning and trying to determine the best method of teaching culture in the language classroom. There are no absolute or fixed conclusions in regard to the latter. The individual teacher is left to their own determination when it comes to helping their students overcome the cultural hurdles in the classroom and in their own dual language lives. This is very much an individual problem that seems to be unique in every case. The problem facing the teacher is how to get the student to get out of the world of translation, which doesn't get the student very far, and into the state where their second language is second nature and automatic. This is where the good teacher really comes 'into their own', but how can the teacher facilitate this change.

The challenge for the teacher is to get the students to relax and forget their personal cultural values and that they are in class. If possible and you have the good fortune to have a mixture of cultures in your class, mix them up so they do not have their fellow countrymen to keep them in their own cultural world and reinforce their feelings. If the students revert to using their native tongue they immediately lose focus. The students like to get involved in activities where there is the need to think and they compete with the other class members. The results are usually better when there are competing teams.

Chapter three

When you were a child the one of the first things you learned was how to get information. If you did not know the name of whatever you were thinking of, you asked questions and used the names of things related to what you wanted until you got the result you needed. You also learned how to give the information to get the answers you wanted by describing things. These skills are not just useful they are vital to us all and we use them constantly in our daily lives. There are no course books or classes that give students help in transferring these necessary skills to the new language. When the students are actively engaged in activities they can re—acquire or transfer these skills to their new language without even realizing they are doing so. They are really surprised with their increased skill level in the new language afterwards but don't know where that skill came from. Immersion weekends are very helpful when the students need to re-acquire these skills.

There is a real need for the students to automatically think in the target language and to have the words they use connected to their feelings the problem facing the teacher is how to get that to happen. Reading the course books alone will never bring this about. The teacher has to get the students moving, interacting with others and while doing so, learn something about the culture and way of life of the target language country. This is where activities really help the learning process as they get the students reacting without thinking first and translating. Any activity that encourages questions and answers is also an excellent thing in the classroom. Questions and answers help the student transfer the early language skills so the students need to be encouraged to ask lots of questions about all aspects of the material presented. Games such as twenty questions, where the players have twenty questions to try to find out the name of what the teacher has chosen for them to discover are especially good. Short stories or articles that illustrate the culture of the target language, the way the people live and relate to each other and society are good as well if the students can read and discuss them. This imprints the culture of the target language as well as making the students aware of the differences.

It is also essential that the students repeatedly use the language and listen frequently to the same thing being presented in the past, perfect, present and future tenses. This will do far more good towards their learning of the Grammar of the target language than just reading the grammar books. This way they learn 'real language', not how to translate text from their own language. The teacher has to keep in mind that the students are there to learn how to communicate with other people and do it well, not to pass written tests on the new language.

The classes have to be fun, people remember what has been presented if they are enjoying being there. This does not mean that progress be limited while everyone just has a good time, the teacher will be judged and evaluated by the students according to their own evaluation of the progress which is, of course, the only real measure of success.

Chapter four

Now we are aware of some of the impediments in teaching English to our foreign students we have to consider how we can succeed in the task we set for ourselves.

Good teaching, regardless of what is being taught, or the teaching location on the face of our world, is the result of making connections. Without a connection with the student we can never achieve our goal of bringing the student from the known and having them accept and understand what is at the time, the unknown.

People can only relate to what has been in their life experience so we have to connect with the student using information and references to known things. The teacher has to be sensitive and make the connection so that they know if the student can relate to what they are trying to convey and understand the material. This is the part that is very much influenced by the cultural differences. The best way to do this is to give the information in stages and ask frequent questions to help determine if the lesson is getting through. The students have to be gently led from their own culture into the cultural understanding that shapes the target language.

Culture influences how we learn and how we teach. Teaching within our own culture is an activity where social and cultural context and the existence of different thinking, learning and instructional styles interact in a very complex fashion. The classroom is a complex socio-cultural environment even when working within our own culture. The age, sex, gender role, expectations, appearance and dress, personal expectations, numerous other role expectations, socio-economic status and the many other characteristics of both the students and teachers are all variables affecting the interactions and so influencing the effectiveness of instruction and the amount of learning which takes place in the classroom. The situation becomes even more complex when students and instructors are from different cultures. Culture influences norms of verbal and non-verbal interaction within the classroom. Even within the North Americas, sub-cultural and socio-economic differences can create vastly different classroom interaction patterns.

A society's educational processes normally display a vast array of thinking styles, learning styles, teaching styles and styles of learning environment. Culture can contribute to making certain styles more prominent than others. Every teacher has his or her own style of teaching, there are different national and cultural academic traditions, and there are often cultural differences in pedagogy. But regardless of styles, traditions and cultures, all good teaching anywhere in the world consists of one thing, which is important, making connections with the students.

Effective teaching requires the use of cognitive, motivational and behavioral supports. And where the language of instruction is the student's second language, good teaching also requires considerable linguistic supports as well. Teachers must utilize and build these supports into their courses, methods of classroom instruction and overall interaction with students. The teacher must repeat the material in different ways and question the students frequently to determine if they have grasped what has been taught to them. It is then advisable to have the students paraphrase the material and report back to the teacher. The material is understood better if the teaching speed is slowed and the language used is simple as well as avoiding slang, idiomatic expressions, and jargon and using the words that the teacher knows the students already understand. It is also advisable to frequently repeat the material and paraphrase what has been said.

Read through the material you are going to teach, before you start the class, then preview and explain the meaning of any new words. It can only be emphasised that any other things that are available to support the material and help the understanding of the students is invaluable, things like maps, photographs and stories in newspapers and magazines.

There is a saying that a picture is worth a thousand words and it is true in the ESL classroom. The value of a good, easily understood story that contains material that is being taught can be equally valuable as well. Movies, slides, CDs are also good teaching aids, such as transparencies and text book illustrations. It is really valuable to be sensitive to the understanding and life experience of the students so that the connections can be made and the material presented in a manner they can understand by building on whatever familiarities you are aware of. You have to be tuned in to the lives of the students so that you can present the material in a way that they can understand. This means that you can use examples and comparisons with things that you know they are familiar with to help reinforce the connection you have made.

The need for student motivation is another thing that has to be stressed. Setting a direction for the students, and maintaining their interest in the course. The teacher also needs to relate to the students in their lives and to keep them excited about what they are learning. It also helps the students if they are well informed with regard to what is expected of them so they are comfortable with the routine and expectations with regard to what is expected in the way of writing, reading, note taking, test writing and so on. Positive reinforcement helps the student's behavioural modification in class so they have minimum negative things to deal with. We should never push the students to learn but rather we should lead them. Our role in their learning process is that of a facilitator who helps them rise to the expectations we have of them while we encourage them and praise them as well as offering rewards for the way they are succeeding.

The exciting thing for us as teachers is the knowing that we are helping the students modify their neural networks and set them up with some different thinking patterns as we help them acquire a new language so their brains are stronger and function better while being more useful as a result of our efforts. Bi-lingual people have more abilities especially with artistic pursuits and music.
There is another thing that we have not covered in these notes and that is the different learning styles of the students. Regardless of cultural background the different learning styles are not universal but there are some distinct characteristics.

Teaching styles

How often have you prepared and given your class then noticed that only a few of your students seem to have grasped what you taught?

This is not uncommon and is caused by the students having different styles of learning.

There are four ways that people learn and the material has to be presented to them all in the manner they understand and grasp to enable them to learn. The styles are quite distinct and unfortunately if you do not give the information to them in their style they will only get some of what you want them to learn.

The styles are as named below with suggestions for addressing the associated problems.

It will already have occurred to you that you yourself have a distinct, personal style of teaching so you have to take that into account and modify your approach to accommodate the student's needs. Firstly there are the:

Auditory Learners.

Students who get a lot out of lectures, verbal explanations, tapes and oral instruction are generally classed as auditory learners. Instructional games for this type of learner are mainly listening based. They include games that involve repetition, dictation, and listening for clues. These games are any games that involve students repeating language they have had demonstrated or written down for them. Chinese Whispers, Jazz Chants, and Karaoke Night are good examples of these kinds of games. If you are you are teaching adults who are more conservative, use a variation of Jazz Chants with a short rhythmic dialog and a metronome, or hand clapping, and emphasize the fluency practice.

Listening Games.

Students studying English in their own country often express concern that they can understand their teacher but not other native speakers. In the language classroom you can practice listening by using tapes or videos with short dialogs for listening games like Vocabulary Scavenger Hunt, which involves trying to locate the necessary vocabulary words on multiple tapes at different listening stations. Jigsaw listening is also an excellent team building game, as the teams send representatives to different listening stations, and then try to reconstruct the story when all the listeners have returned to the team. These kinds of games also help students learn how to make use of TV and radio broadcasts in English to practice on their own.

Quiz building games.

Quiz building games are an excellent way of learning because question and answer games embody all of the seven aspects of learning.

Games like Jeopardy, grammar knockout type games and listening memory games are great for auditory learners of any level, since you can go from basic questions like spelling and definitions, to more challenging ones like asking for a word to be used in a sentence, explanation of grammar rules, or cultural trivia.

Another set of games to teach auditory learners are story and sentence building games such as Madlibs, either the store bought, or self made, where the students fill in words to make funny and nonsensical stories. These types of games require excellent listening skills as the student keeps track of what will be required for the next turn, plus they usually finish with a verbal recap of the finished story or sentence allowing students to check their understanding.

Visual Learners.

Visual learners are students who prefer to read quietly and make good use of any illustrations that go with the texts. They will generally prefer to be taught with written instructions and will benefit from the teacher and students acting out situations, watching demonstrations or scenarios in videos. If you have a student who seems to retain what they read better than what they hear then that student is an example of a visual learner. There are many games or activities that work with this kind of student, as well as helping non-visual learners make the most of visual cues that can also help them learn and use English.

Board games.

There are plenty of commercial board games that can be used in the classroom, but you can also make your own. "Folder games" involve making a game board, often based on commercial boards, and using them to practice grammar, vocabulary, phonics, and spelling.

Picture games.

These games include anything played with pictures as their main starting point. Playing games with flashcards, or adapting the game Jeopardy to use picture prompts is one example. Another one that is a lot of fun with advanced students is picture captioning or comic strip re-writes. If you use comics from different countries, you can get into some very sophisticated discussions about what constitutes humor in different countries. Many students get to a certain level of advanced English, and then plateau. The reason for this is that they have a difficult time when situations become abstract and involves taking their English outside of academic or basic survival situations. Studying humor through these visual games can help to bridge that gap.

Reading games.

Reading is an essential skill for all students and works especially well with visual learners. Language games like Reading Treasure Hunts with color-coded pencils, where the students look for particular parts of speech or vocabulary, teaches skimming as well as reviewing grammar and or vocabulary. Then Important Sentences with Watermelon, where teams send a representative to put sentences in order, helps with summarizing, working under pressure, and team building. This game has the added bonus of being suitable for tactile learners as well.

Tactile and Kinesthetic Learners

Tactile and Kinesthetic learners are usually the students who just don't get what you're trying to teach in a traditional lecture or worksheet based lesson. Kinesthetic learners take in information best when they use their whole bodies to practice the exercises. Tactile learners are also physical learners, but they are more likely to learn things from model building or hands on instruction.

There were studies done in the 1980s that revealed the majority of the students were Tactile or Kinesthetic learners. Bearing this in mind one realizes the importance of integrating physical aspects into the lessons. You will therefore have to find activities that involve whole body responses such as having the students moving objects around and touching things as a part of the activity. There are three distinct kinds of activities or games that have these elements.

Touch games.

One good game in this category involves having items inside a bag. The students have to touch an object in the bag and then say what it is they have touched. This improves vocabulary. To make it more difficult for the advanced students they can try to describe the item and then the rest of the class tries to discover what it is and name it.

Spatial games.

This kind of activity involves rearranging items or people. The game of Charades is a good example of this type of activity and as an alternative you can try having all the students except one having a card with either a word or a punctuation mark on it. The student without a card will then try to rearrange the others so that they create a properly punctuated sentence by using as many of the others as possible

Craft games.

These are any kind of game or activity where the students actually assemble something. Lego is a good example of this type of activity. If you do not have Lego available then you can find a substitute. To make the activity more interesting and a greater learning aid you can include the need for the students to negotiate to get the pieces they need to complete the task. This increases the learning because it includes an auditory component

None of these activities will solve all of the problems you will encounter when giving English classes but they are an excellent way of addressing the different learning styles of the students. The activities serve to relax the students, putting them at ease while stimulating their senses. They not only address the individual problems but they also serve to broaden the learning styles of the students involved.

Teaching pronunciation

Spoken English is quite different to many other languages because it is a stress timed, rhythmic language with variation of intonation and stress being used to give greater meaning to what is being said.

Students find these this ability difficult to grasp and this also give problems with student comprehension because their ears are not tuned to catch the modification of the pronunciation of the function words in the sentences to maintain the rhythm of the spoken language.

The English language has an extensive vocabulary because for thousands of years as maritime nations have been attracted to the temperate island and have left some of their language there. The British were also a maritime nation and colonised many lands. The people who returned from the other lands also brought back words and expressions that were then added to the language and quite often with their original pronunciation.

The most difficult aspect to master in English is the unstressed pronunciation of all the function words in the sentences. Most non native speakers use syllabic languages so they will stress these function words strongly and disturb the normal flow and rhythm of the words.

The importance of these words is not their number or their size, but in the frequency of their use. The ten most frequently used words in English are all function words. These words make up 25 % of all that is written or spoken in English and they are: *the, of and, to, a, in, that, it, I and I.*
Altogether there are actually sixty monosyllabic function words in English as well as another 20 duo-syllabic ones.
They actually use these relatively few words make up over 30 percent of the language!!
To put it another way, nearly every third word is a function word.
It is an unfortunate fact that these function words are the very words that the students really mispronounce because they over-pronounce them.
If you and your students really wish to improve your English the way to do so is by them learning to pronounce these function words correctly and automatically.

Homophones

The following is a list of very common contractions with words that have a different spelling and meaning but exactly the same pronunciation sound.

You're	your	yore
it's	its	
we're	weir	
they're	their,	there
aren't	aunt	
we've	weave	
I'd	eyed	
he'd	heed	
we'd	weed	
I'll	isle	
you'll	Yule	
he'll	heel,	heal
we'll	wheel	
here's	hears	
there's	theirs	
what's	watts	

The rhythm.

English has several levels of stress on certain syllables in each sentence to help convey the meaning. Most of the other languages use less with the verb being used as the main means of giving the meaning of the sentence.

In English there is a stressed syllable approximately every point six (0.6) of a second and the main point of the sentence is expressed by giving extra stress to one syllable in one of the words. (Sentence stress) The stressed syllable in the content words, every 0.6 of a second, is constant, regardless of the number of words used in the sentence. This means that the function words have, out of necessity, their pronunciation modified to get them to fit in. Some are shortened or clipped and often are pronounced joined together like they are one word. This gives foreign people great difficulty grasping what has been said because their ears are tuned to hear each syllable pronounced as an equal part of the sentence. The content words are the words that give the real meaning of what the sentence expresses. They are usually the Nouns, Verbs and sometimes the Adjectives.

For example:

Fig. 1.

!	0.6sec.	!	0.6sec	!	0.6sec.	!

COWS   **EAT**   **GRASS.**

The sentence really needs more words to give the full meaning so they are added between the content words. These are the function words. They are squeezed in between the content words but they do not change the rhythm.

Fig.1a.

!	0.6sec.	!	0.6sec	!	0.6sec.	!

       COWS   **EAT**   **GRASS.**

The **COWS**   **EAT**   the **GRASS**.

The **COWS**   will **EAT**   the **GRASS**.

The **COWS**   will have **EAT**en   all of the **GRASS.**

The pronunciation of the function words is modified when speaking so that the rhythm of the language is maintained so it will sound like this.

The ***COWS***   *'ll'ave* ***EAT***   *en alluvthu* ***GRASS***

SCHWA

Reduced phrases.

The rhythm and stress patterns of English force certain phrases to be reduced.

PHRASE.	CONTEXT	TRANSCRIPTION.
Want to.	She didn't want to believe me.	wana.
I don't know.	I don't know.	ardeno.
How did you?	How did you do it?	howdgea.

And so on.

You note that the vowel sound in the unstressed words is reduced to a sound that has no quality of an a, e, I, o, u. The vowel sound is neither open, nor closed, fronted or backed, rounded nor spread. It is pronounced with the tongue and lips totally relaxed as if you are asleep or daydreaming.
Air is blown through the mouth and the vocal chords vibrate. This vowel is called Schwa.
It is the most frequently pronounced vowel sound in the English language yet it has no letter to represent it in the English Alphabet.
Unfortunately this is almost never taught to native speakers and even less so to English Foreign Language students.
Research has determined that Schwa occurs more than 34% of the time in spoken English.
The Scwa is undoubtedly the most important element to learn to be able to reproduce the correct rhythm and un-stress patterns of English.

The rhythm of the language is very distinctive as these diagrams indicate. If one were to draw a diagram of the pronunciation of a foreign sentence it would look like this with all the syllables being nearly equal in stress.

As vacas que comeram toda a erva. (Brazilian Portuguese)

Here is another example of comparison.

Eng. The girl turned the radio off.
o O o o O o

Fr. La jeune fille a ferme la radio
O OOOOO OOO

all of the syllables have more or less equal stress in Brazilian Portuguese, French, Spanish, German, Italian, Chinese and many other languages.

Intonation

The main change in intonation is to give added impact to the meaning accented by the stressed syllables. In many languages there is a change of intonation at the end of the sentence. Many languages change the intonation of some of the words but only slightly when compared to English. The intonation changes in English are quite pronounced and foreigner's think that native speakers of English are emotional or excited when they are just speaking normally.

The vowel sounds of the English language are also different as they have more than one sound, long and short. They have a short sound in most cases but when they are positioned in front of a consonant that is followed by the letter 'e' the sound changes to the same sound as the name of the letter like this.

Rat. Rate. Sit. Site. Rot. Rote and so on.
The vowel sounds are pronounced with the sound shaped by the position of the speaker's Lips and the Tongue.
Some of the sounds of the English vowels are made at the front of the mouth, some in the middle and the others at the rear of the mouth.
The greater number of different vowel and diphthong sounds that are used are also very difficult for the students to get used to as well.
English has far more vowel and diphthongs sounds than most other languages and the positioning of the lips and tongue, combined with the respiration are vital for getting the correct pronunciation. Below are some diagrams that illustrate the tongue positions for the vowel sounds:

Vowel sounds diagrams.

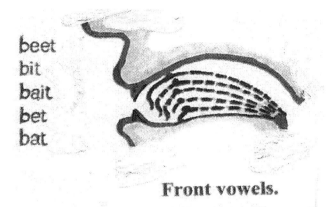

beet
bit
bait
bet
bat

Front vowels.

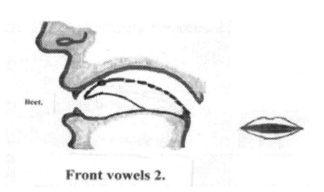

Beet.

Front vowels 2.

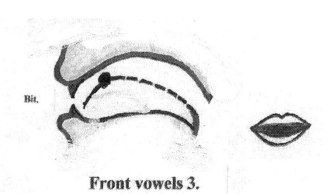

Bit.

Front vowels 3.

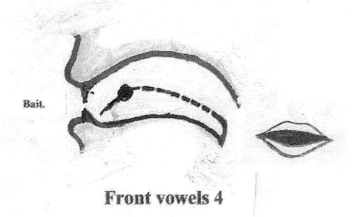

Bait.

Front vowels 4

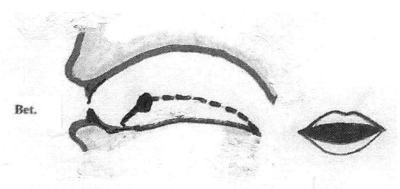

Bet.

Front vowels 5

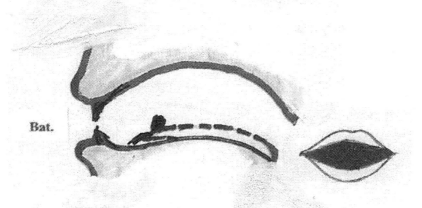

Bat.

Front vowels 6

bird
to
fun

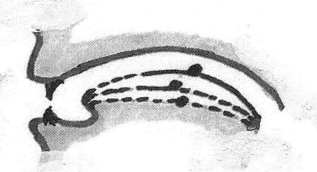

Central vowels.

Bird.

Central vowels 2.

To.

Central vowels 3.

Fun.

Central vowels 4.

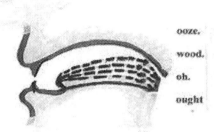

ooze.

wood.

oh.

ought

Back vowels.

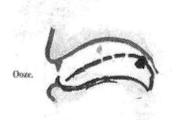

Ooze.

Back vowels 2.

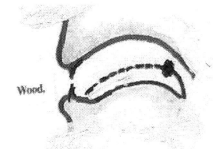

Wood.

Back vowels 3.

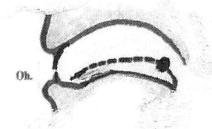

Oh.

Back vowels 4.

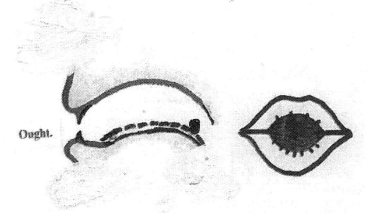

Ought.

Back vowels 5.

The English native speaker has flexible lips and as you can see the tongue is used to shape the sound of the vowels.

If you can practice the pronunciation often you should find that the ability to pronounce the words will come to be much easier with time.

Intonation

One noticeable change in intonation is at the end of the sentence and many languages, as does English, change the intonation of some of the words.
In English the intonation of the last syllable of a sentence varies if the sentence is a question.
If the question does not demand and answer the intonation falls.
If an answer is necessary, the intonation rises.

Pauses and stress changes

Students also have difficulty with the placing of the pauses and the stress, if any, and are unaware of the considerable change they make to the meaning of what is said.

For example.

John, said the **Professor**, is an **idiot**.
Now if the pauses are moved we get.
John said, the **Professor** is an **idiot.**
The music is very loud.
The **music** is **very** loud.
The **music is** very **loud.**
The **music** is very **loud**

Cognates and False Cognates.

English, like all languages, is a living language and the meanings of many words have changed over time. These changes are still happening. Many of the words in English have their roots in other languages. The path they took to arrive in English may have included several other languages before arriving in English.

The meanings of words that changed languages over time very often changed meanings as well. When learning another language one often comes across a word that is used in English as well as the other language. This does not mean that the meaning is the same in both languages however. Quite often the meaning might prove to be opposite.

The ones with the same meaning are Cognates and then others are obviously the False Cognates. These are a few examples in French, German and Brazilian Portuguese.

French English False Cognates

Engrosser (F) **vs Engross** (E) **Engrosser** (F) is a familiar verb meaning *to knock up, get someone pregnant.*

Engross (E) means *absorber, captiver*. **Luxure** (F) **vs Luxury** (E)

Luxure (F) = *lust*.E **Luxury** (E) = *luxe*.F

Lac (F) **vs Lack** (E) **Lac** (F) is a large body of water—*lake*.

Lack (E) is a deficiency or absence—*un manque*

Laid (F) is an adjective meaning *ugly*.

Laid (E) is the past tense of the English verb to lay: he laid his

Briefcase on the table—she was laid on the ground

German Cognates

debut **s Debüt** decadence **Dekadenz**
decadent **decadent** decimal **Dezimal**, December **Dezember**
deck **Deck** (*nautical, bus*)

German False Cognates

bald soon **bekommen** to get, receive **Biskuit** sponge cake/dough)

Portuguese Cognates.

Analise In Portuguese	Analysis in English
Analogia. In Portuguese.	Analogy in English
Animado in Portuguese.	Animate in English

False Cognates.

compromisso. In Portuguese.	Commitment. In English
educado. In Portuguese.	Polite. In English
esperto. In Portuguese	intelligent, sly. In English

Teaching Writing

Teaching the students to write in their new language is an essential part of the teaching how to use the new language. There is no question that the pen is mightier than the sword and the ability to express one's self clearly is a tremendous asset. Written record of what you write in office memos and other business idea and plan creation sessions are durable, and can surface at some time in the future and you get the credit for your brain child.

It is a good idea to start the students writing as soon as possible. In the early stages when the language is very basic. It helps to have the students practice by taking short dictations. This gets them used to writing, remember the spelling of the new words as well as acquire some understanding of the structure of the sentences. This practice also helps the students gain a working knowledge of the use of punctuation marks as well.

Later on homework is a good opportunity to practice writing. Students can be asked to read a short story or an article in a magazine or newspaper and then put the story into their own words. This is an excellent way to practice expression as well as give a good indication of the student's comprehension of the new language.

Writing Clearly.

Since business writing is practical application of language, an effective business style is not fancy but functional. It's simple and straightforward. Some writers deliberately stuff their writing with high-flown terminology and elaborate phrases, thinking that such style will make them seem more intelligent or sophisticated. Don't make that mistake. Complicated writing is often confusing, and may make you seem confused. On the other hand, if your writing is lucid, you will come across as a lucid thinker. It follows that if you really want to impress your most discerning associates, you will begin by making your writing clear and clearly understood without too many opportunites for ambiguities.

Choosing Clear Wording.

In selecting words, it's worth remembering the difference between the dictionary meaning of a word (it's **denotation**) and the associative meanings or range of suggestions it calls up (it's **connotation**). A thesaurus is a very usefull tool but the words listed as synonyms in a thesaurus do not always mean the same thing. Some words have positive or negative associations, while others are more neutral. For example, the adjective *strong-minded* is grouped in a thesaurus with *strong-willed, hardy, firm, resolute, dogged, determined.* But what executive wouldn't prefer being called "strong-minded," "resolute." Or "firm," to "dogged"? Take care, therefore, that the subtle shadings of the words you choose give the message you want.

Use Everyday, Plain Words.

Through the centuries, English speakers have adopted and adapted a great many words from other languages, especially French and Latin. Yes the most common words in the English language are usually the oldest and have their roots in Anglo Saxon English. The words children first learn are derived from the same Anglo Saxon stock used since before AD 1000. Whether we recognize the reason or not, we usually choose these words for our conversations, since they seem most natural. Plain English words are also generally short – another good reason to use them.

By contrast, a lot of foreign derivatives, even if they have been in our vocabulary for years, still seem less natural. This is not to suggest that you *never* use an unusual or long word. Used occasionally, an uncommon word can be effective. Nevertheless, while a string of them will make your writing seem artificial or pretentious, they can however be effective when used sparingly.

French derivatives, for example, may give an aura of class. Every copywriter knows that you sell a fine wine by its bouquet rather than its smell, and a perfume by its fragrance. Every ad for upper level real estate seems to mention residences with foyers rather than houses with entrance halls. Even if you consider yourself a plain "meat and potatoes" kind of person, you surely would feel inelegant at a restaurant if you asked for pig rather than pork (from porc) or cow rather than beef (boeuf). The point is that in business writing you may choose French based words of expressions for a particular effect, but you will generally avoid a lot of them if you don't want to seem phony. Notice the natural, direct quality of the words in the second column, compared to those in the first:

French Derivatives.	Plain English.
Request.	ask
Desire.	Want.
Assist.	Help.
Endeavor.	Try.
Dine.	Eat.
Pursue.	Follow.
Commence.	Begin.

You should also avoid a lot of Latinate words. Even if you have never taken Latin, you will be able to recognize Latinate words by the attached prefixes (such as *pro, anti, ante, sub, super, ad, ex, con, pre*) or supefixes (*ism, ent, ate, ise, or ize, tion*). Such attach-ments are useful in science, since they add precision to the description of structures and processes. (think of common scientific verbs like *evaporate, crystallize, react, ingest, absorb,* and *liquefy*; or noun forms like *condensation, magnetism,* and *coagulation*). Even in a formal but non-scientific context, the occasional Latinate word can add a feeling of scholarly dignity.

The trouble comes with too much: writing that is full of Latinate words is dense and difficult to understand. Business people who want to appear scientific often mistakenly fill their writing with unnecessary Latinisms, and nearly kill their meaning (to say nothing of their readers). Unfortunately, the Latinate disease is spreading, but you should try not to catch it. American English often full of Latinate words.

1. **Be wary of newly formed** *ize* **words**. (or ise words, if using british rather than American spelling); for example, *incrementalize, sensitize, finalize, operationalize, optionalize*. Although words like *maximize* and *minimize* have taken such firm root in our vocabulary that they are unlikely to be weeded out, it's a good idea to use plainer substitutes when you can.

Latinism	Plain English.
Finalize.	Finish, complete.
Operationalize.	Start.
Maximize.	Increase.
Optionalize.	Allow choice.
Prioritize.	Rank.
Utilize.	Use.

2. **Avoid lengthy nouns that end in** ion **and a formed from verbs**, especially when the verb has an ize ending. Notice how the wording in the three columns becomes progressively more complex — and weaker — through the use of Latinisms.

Plain.	Latinate Verb.	Noun Form.
Order.	Systemize.	Systemization.
Toughen.	Desensitize.	Desensitization.
Start.	Operationalize.	Operiationalization.
Make aware.	Familiarize.	Familiarization.

Be Specific.

To keep readers from having to second-guess you, be as exact in your words as you can. You often replace vague, "all purpose" verbs like *involve, concern,* and *affect* with ones that are not as open to interpretation. In addition, use specific names, dates, times, and amounts to increase the clarity of the message. Admittedly, when you are referring to a group, it may be impractical to list each member or item. When you have a choice, however, be specific rather than general:

Poor.	*We are concerned about the environmental factors that affect two provinces.*
Acceptable.	**We are worried about (or we are studying) the acid rain which threatens the lakes of Ontario and Quebec.**
Poor choice.	*Management is concerned that your costing expert be involve in the planning process for the renovation.*
Acceptable.	**Hugh Wills wants your costing expert, Sheila Moore, to do estimates for the renovation.**

Poor choice.	*Since you were involved in the report, I'd be interested in knowing about it sometime.*
Acceptable.	**Since you prepared the report, please call me next week to discuss it.**
Poor choice.	Rogers had a significant rise in sales recently.
Acceptable.	**Roger's sales have increased ten per cent in the last six months.**

Remember also that the pronoun *this* or *it* must refer to a specific noun. Writers often use one or the other in a vague way, so that it is unclear what exactly the reference is. Here is an example:

We completed the project this week by working until late Friday night and by bringing in an extra typist. This pleased our client.

What does *this* refer to? Revising the phrase to *this completion* or *this extra work* makes the meaning clearer.

Avoid Jargon.

Most areas of knowledge, trades, professions and disciplines have a terminology, which helps experts communicate with each other. The special terms allow them to say quickly and precisely what they mean, without having to resort each time to definitions or explanations. Scientists in particular rely upon technical terms, as a doctor does when describing a patient's medical condition to a colleague. The difficulty arises when people unnecessarily use jargon — complicated or unfamiliar terms — perhaps in an attempt to appear scientific or sophisticated. Rather than clarifying an issue, they obscure it. The teacher who wrote the following bit of jargon may not have been trying to appear sophisticated, but certainly was obscuring the message.

Poor choice. *Harry often exhibits overtly aggressive tendencies in interactive situations with his peer group, especially in extra-curricular activities.*

What the teacher could have said was:

Better. Harry often fights with his classmates, especially outside the classroom.

People in business sometimes make the mistake of cluttering their writing with jargon to demonstrate their "insider knowledge." Instead of following this approach, remember that the brightest minds are those that can simplify a complicated issue, not complicate a simple one. The guideline is straightforward: use specialized terms if they are a kind of short form, making communication easier. Avoid jargon when plain English will do.

Writing Clear Sentences.

Writing clear sentences is not only a matter of choosing plain, clear wording; it also entails using correct grammar and punctuation. What "correct" means is sometimes open to dispute. Acceptable grammar and punctuation are really conventions or customary practices; the way educated people speak and write over a period of years and throughout a wide area becomes known as "standard" English. Following a standard is useful in business writing but the standard will be subject to constant change. It enables people from a variety of areas and backgrounds to understand one another readily. Most of the rules of grammar and punctuation are a way of making sense, of communicating efficiently. Maybe extra classes will prove necessary to explain the important rules of grammar and punctuation, providing examples and exercises. If your knowledge of rules is scant or rusty, refer to them. You can also take advantage of your ears and eyes.

Listen to what you Say. Practice reading your work out loud in a firm voice. Listen carefully. Children learn the language not by rules but by ears; writers also need to use their ears. If something doesn't "sound right" to you, chances are it won't to your reader. If you find yourself stumbling over a sentence, try reconstructing it in a simpler way. If you have to catch your breath several times in the middle, the sentence is probably too long. Break it up. Reading out loud, although it takes more time than a silent skim, will make you a better critic.

Reading aloud also helps you to catch errors such as typos, agreement problems, and spelling mistakes because it forces you to slow down and really see (and hear) what is on the page.

Do a spot check. Eyes are a second line of defense against sentence errors. Try to remember the kinds of mistakes you made in the past and check especially for them. If you learn to spot your mistakes when you are editing, you will soon find that you make fewer of them.

Creating Clear Paragraphs.

Paragraphs are difficult to define because they have so many shapes and sizes. They are needed, however, to help the reader follow the development and shift of ideas. These guidelines for paragraphing will help you maintain a sense of clarity and order in your writing:

Create a new paragraph for a change in idea or topic. Paragraphs develop and frame ideas. By creating a new paragraph, you signal to a reader that you have finished developing one idea or an aspect of it and are switching to another. Of course, it is possible to outline several ideas in a single paragraph, for example, if you are briefly stating the reasons for some action. If you discuss an idea at any length in a paragraph, however, you should create a new paragraph when you move on to another idea.

Make the first sentence the main point. It is important that your writing has a sense of direction. The human mind prefers order to disorder, and always struggles to make sense out of an array of facts. If you immediately provide that order by stating the key points first, the reader can more readily fit together the particulars that follow. The assimilation of information is easier.

Read the following paragraph. Notice that the main idea is at the end. Although this indirect order is perfectly reasonable, the busy or impatient reader will more readily catch the drift of the paragraph if the last sentence becomes the first one.

From 1975 to 1990 in Baytown, the percentage of our citizens over 65 years doubled, and demographic analysis suggests that this trend will continue. Many seniors live lonely, isolated lives. Over one third subsist on small pensions and living below the poverty line. Our municipal government should assume more responsibility for identifying the particular needs of our seniors and coordinating services to them. We need a coordinator of Seniors' Services for Baytown to help improve the quality of life of our older people.

Admittedly, not all paragraphs in good prose have a beginning key point or topic sentence; nor does every topic sentence have to appear at the beginning. In creating a persuasive argument for example, you may want to lead indirectly to the key idea by starting with particular facts and later pulling them together with a general statement. Yes, for most business writing, begin each paragraph with the main point. Do a quick check on the sequence of paragraph beginnings in your writing. If you get a clear idea of the line of your thinking, your writing will likely seem well ordered and logical to the readers.

Vary paragraph lengths. The trend in business writing is to short paragraphs. They look less dense than long ones and are more inviting to read. Follow this trend and avoid long paragraphs. When you see a chain of long paragraphs (over eight or ten lines), try splitting some at an appropriate spot. On the other hand, a string of one sentence or two sentence paragraphs can make your writing seem choppy and undeveloped. Clearly, a single sentence paragraph can effectively begin a letter to call attention to an idea, and short paragraphs are appropriate for news releases and brief correspondence. However for reports or other complex discussion, the ideas need more development if they are to be accepted. Typical ways to develop an idea in a paragraph are by:

* Illustrating the idea.
* Classifying the parts.
* Revealing cause or effect.
* Giving a solution to a problem.
* Comparing or contrasting with another idea.

Of course, you may want to take more than a paragraph for any of these methods of expansion, but at least, see that your paragraphs go beyond a simple point to a discussion of that point. If readers have commented that you need to explain your idea more fully, the list above provides good ways to do so.

Good writing in business usually comprises a range of paragraph lengths, from short (two or three sentences) to moderately long (seven or eight sentences), with most paragraphs somewhere in-between. In considering your own paragraphs, try for variety; it's as much the spice of writing as of life.

Keep the focus. Some paragraphs may not seem focused, even though the sentences are all on topic. The reason may be that they are constantly shifting the grammatical subject. Notice the difference in these two paragraphs (the grammatical subjects are in bold):

Poor choice.

*Business **analysts** have noted the different ways manages operate. Sometimes all the **decisions** are made by a manager, and **employees** are given orders or procedures to follow. The **success** of this kind of manager is not long term, since leaders are not developed as potential successors. The opposite **type** is the manager who avoids making decisions, tending to delay by forming committees and requesting endless studies. **Managers** of this sort are also not effective. **Employees** find themselves between these extremes with managers who encourage their participation in planning. **Responsibility** for making the final decision remains in the boss's hands. **These** are effective managers.*

Much better.

As business analysts have noted, modern managers have different ways of operating. Some tend to make all the decisions, giving employees orders and procedures to follow. In the long tem they are ineffective since they do not develop leaders who can succeed them. Other managers avoid making decisions, tending to form committees and request endless studies. They are also ineffective. In-between these extremes are managers who encourage employees to participate in planning, but who take final responsibility for decisions. These managers are effective.

The second paragraph is clearer and easier to read because it is better focused; more of the grammatical subjects are the same — managers.

You may wonder: If the grammatical subject is always the same, how can a paragraph not be boring? Here are two tips, both followed in the second paragraph above:

* Use stand in words. These are **pronouns** and **synonyms** of the subject.
* Put something in front of the subject. Although the grammatical subject is most often at the beginning, it can also come later in the sentence. Putting a word, phrase, or clause in front of the subject ("As business analysts have noted," "in the long term," "in between these two extremes") makes the subject less noticeable.

Link the ideas. Some words and phrases have a linking function, signaling to the reader the relationship between sentences and parts of a sentence. They act as both glue to the logic and guide to the transitions between ideas. Correct use of common linking words and phrases listed below will help make your paragraphs more clear and coherent.

Clear writing is not attained by using a large vocabulary and long words.

Most people in their daily lives only use a vocabulary of approximately six hundred words. The exceptions are when one needs to use the common place words that are pertinent to the discipline, business or professions. So the rule is definitely keep it simple and clearly understandable.

When you are at this stage of the student's development you may start to notice the influence of the student's native culture. The culture of the student really influences their ability to express themselves freely. The Chinese have an aversion to changing text that they have read. They have been taught that it is not possible to improve on the thinking of the original writer or expression of the original text. Some other cultures also have this problem in varying degrees.

If the writer experiences writer's block it can be helped by getting them to just write anything that comes to mind and then editing the results afterwards. The act of just writing freely often unblocks the writer. Effective editing can usually make something of what is written.

It is very necessary to get the students to understand the need to edit the work at least three times and then have someone else read the results. The other person will notice things that the writer misses and can be a great help by asking question of the writer to help clarify what the writer is saying.

We do not notice our own mistakes or bad habits because to us they are the way to express things and seem to be right to us. Another person may need help or changes to the phrasing to help them understand what is written.
There are many websites on the Internet, many of them written by the English departments in various universities that offer guidance for writers. It can help students tremendously to have this additional help.

General information.

The English language has an extensive vocabulary because for thousands of years maritime people from many places in the world, such as the Phoenicians in five thousand BC. had been attracted to the nice, green, temperate climate land. The migration of various peoples continued throughout the ages. The British were also a maritime nation and colonised many places around the globe. The travelers and colonists returned with words from the languages they had encountered in their travels and they became part of the English language. Many of these words retained their spelling and sometimes their original pronunciation. This can be very confusing to a student. It is confusing to some of the English speaking nations around the world such as the Americans. The Americans have many words which are spelled differently and pronounced very differently with the stress being placed on a different syllable from the British English.

One of the reasons for this is that English really had no set rules for Grammar until the middle of the seventeen hundreds and the letters had very different forms as well. The S's looked more like f's for a start. Robert Lowth was the first man to publish a book entitled "Introduction to English Grammar" in 1762.

The "Oxford Dictionary" which was published in 1859 firmed up the rules and pronunciation as well as giving much more explicit rules for the Grammar. There have been many words added to the language since 1900 and the pronunciation has been further modified. One of the reasons for this was the class consciousness that developed around speech. Many of the words were created because of the rise in science and technology while many others had Greek or Latin roots.

Why is syllable stress so important in English? This was explained by giving the results of research that English speakers appear to store vocabulary with stress patterns, so a stress mistake can throw a conversation off track, especially if the speaker's control of English vowel sounds is uncertain. Therefore, **the more frequently speakers misuse stress, the more effort listeners have to make to understand what they say**.

Not knowing the importance of syllable stress in English, many students tend to ignore stress patterns of English words. They randomly put stress in any one of the syllables in a word, and sometimes such a stress mistake can cause its meaning changed. For example, a student once said, "The movie I saw yesterday was TERrific." In the word "terrific," he put the stress on the first syllable, rather than the second one; therefore, what we heard was not "terRIfic" but in our minds we think we heard "TERrified," for we listeners usually get the meaning of a word based on its stress pattern.

Another common problem that our students have with English word rhythm is that they tend to give each syllable almost the same strength, length, and pitch. Probably because stress in each syllable in their language is equally strong, they treat English words in the same way. They seem not to know how to weaken and reduce unstressed syllables. A very good example is the word "CHOcolate." Many students say "CHO CO LATE," which is apparently influenced by the rhythm of their native language. In English, a very important characteristic that our students often miss is that vowels in unstressed syllables are mostly reduced to a short central vowel as the vowels reduced in the second and third syllable of "CHOcolate." It is the vowel reduction that makes the difference between stressed and unstressed syllables very clear in English and it is pointed out that "clarity of the vowel is a particularly difficult concept for many students since in their languages all vowels are spoken in a full, clear way. This problem, therefore, deserves more of our attention in the teaching of English word rhythm.

When teaching a new word, the teacher needs to teach its stress pattern as well. The teacher can emphasize stressed syllables by using various visual effects. There are several possibilities and it does not really matter which the teacher chooses provided that he is consistent.

It is also important that the teacher explains the differences in the syllable stress patterns of English and American English. Americans stress a different syllable.

Examples: terRIfic ter**ri**fic ter′ <u>ri</u> fic ter ri fic ter ri fic terrific terrific

They grow flowers in the **green**house.
(a glass building which protects plants from bad weather.)
There are many flowers in the green **house**. This vastly different to a green colored home.

The difference between stressed and unstressed syllables in the English language is much greater than in most other languages. This is the case for stress patterns in sentences and words. To native English speaker the rhythm of many languages (especially French, Spanish, Italian, Brazilian Portuguese, Japanese, Czech, and Cantonese) sounds mechanically regular and rapid series of bursts of sound all of about equal size and force like machine gun fire. English pronounced with such a rhythm sounds extremely rapid and is very difficult to understand.

A description of a French sentence, for example is that it would appear like a group of soldiers of equal size marching along in a line and at a constant double cadence.
English on the other hand would appear more like a disorganized family of various sized people walking in more of a jumbled group.

The following diagrams illustrate the difference between English and many other

Languages.

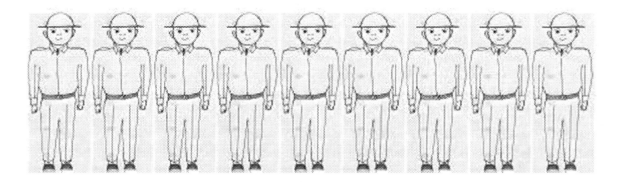

Syllable rhythm of sylabic languages.

Syllable rhythm of an English sentence.

American English

Immigrants from Southeastern England began arriving on the North American continent in the early 1600's. By the mid-1800's, 3.5 million immigrants had left the British Isles for North America.

The American English language is characterized by archaisms (words that changed meaning in Britain, but remained in the colonies) together with innovations in vocabulary (borrowing from the French and Spanish who were also settling in North America). Noah Webster was the most vocal about the need for an American national identity with regards to the American English language. He wrote an American spelling book, *The Blueback Speller*, in 1788 and changed several spellings from British English (colour became color, theatre became theater, etc.) In 1828, he published his famous *American Dictionary of the English Language.*

Dialects in the United States resulted from different waves of immigration of English speakers, contact with other languages, and the slave trade, which had a profound impact on African American English. A dialectal study was done in the 1920s and the findings are published in the *Linguistics Atlas of the U.S. and Canada.*

Some suggested class activities

Twenty Questions.

In this activity the objective is for the team or person to ask questions to find out what the object the teacher has written on the card in their hand.
The questions are limited to twenty and if the object is discovered the team or person is awarded one point. If they fail the point is awarded to the opposing team or person.

Pipes.

This activity is aimed at developing both leadership and co-operation because the activity is both competitive as well getting the students acting as a team. It needs some equipment and some preparation is needed.
This activity needs two buckets and about three pieces of plastic pipe that have been split along the centre line so you have six pieces of trough.
You also need fifty or so balls that will fit into the split pieces of pipe and run freely.

The players are divided into two teams that have been given three of the troughs and half of the available balls.

The teams start some distance from the buckets, as far as is practically possible.

The teacher gives the start signal and then one of each teams players place a ball in the first length of trough.

Then another team member is supposed to place the next piece of trough under the end of the first trough and catch the ball as it runs along and out of the trough.

Another team member will then place their trough under the end of the second trough to continue the progress of the ball.

If the ball is dropped the ball has to be re-started from the beginning again.

The object of the activity is to get as many of the balls as is possible into the team's bucket within the available, allotted time.

Go for a walk.

The objective of this activity is to get the students talking about and describing as well as questioning the things they see along the way. They are to be encouraged to ask questions about the things they see.
It is better if the students are split up into teams of four or five persons. At the start of the walk, one of each of the teams has a teacher as leader and they are given a ball to hold. This person is supposed to talk and make certain that the others in the team respond. When the ball holder cannot continue talking they hand the ball to another team member and they take over the responsibility of leading the group and talking.

Eat a Breakfast meal.

This activity will reinforce knowing the names of the various foods available as well as developing co-operation.

Before the meal is started it helps reach the objective if some of the students are prepared as follows:-

One student has a glove placed on one hand and they are not allowed to use that hand.

One of the students is blindfolded so they are blind and have to ask and have others take care of the things they need.

The meal is taken like any other Breakfast where the students have to ask each other to pass the foods and drinks they need, such as Bread, Butter, Marmalade, Jam etc.

It is better if there is a choice of drinks such as Tea, Coffee, Juices as well as Milk.

The handicapped ones have to ask someone to help them spread their butter and help in

What other ways that seem to be necessary.

Find the word.

Divide the students into two teams.

Sit the student teams some distance apart facing each other.

The teacher needs two assistants who have to have a chalk or white board each.

The two assistants each stand behind one of the teams.

The teacher has one of the assistants hold up their board with a word written on it behind the team they are standing behind.

Their team can then ask questions to try to discover what the word is. The opposing team who able to read the word, do their best to answer any questions asked by the other team members as they attempt to discover what the word is.

Comprehension practice.

Give each of the students a short text that they read and then they take turns in putting the text into their own words. The other students can ask questions to help them understand the meaning of the text is about.

Verb Tenses.

Make up a list of common use Verbs and have the students Take turns making up sentences in the Past, Present, Future and Perfect tenses,

Conversation and Culture practice.

Have one of the students read a short text that contains some cultural aspects such as items that are related to work, social life, family life, marriage and courtship, etc
Then have a group discussion on the differences between their country and the one that the text refers to.

Board games.

If the students can understand the game that is being played it is good for them to participate because the game distracts them from their native cultural roots and the conversation flows more freely.

Scrabble is a particularly good game for the students to play because it also improves their spelling and vocabulary.

Persuasion.

Students try to persuade other students to buy their product, vote for them, or take their point of view in pairs on a given topic. Sounds simple, however you may find students do not have much to say and the conversation is forced or fizzles out. For example if you tell students to discuss their dream home you may find that many students do not have much to say and are not too motivated. The activity is likely to come to an end very soon.

The problem is that the students do not have a real reason to communicate and the setting is artificial. However if you give a compelling reason for the students to speak and to listen you will find the conversation flows more readily. Use this persuasion technique to generate a reason to communicate and stimulate the students. You can discuss any topic with this activity. It is ideal for special subjects as it is for general language.

Here is a detailed example using the topic talking about your dream home. It is better if at first you brainstorm with the class about ideal features for a dream home. With lower intermediate students jot down new vocabulary words the class come up with as they call out their ideas. Specify the type of information that is needed such as location, proximity to services, environment, size, grounds, extra features such as pool or gym, parking, architectural style, whether modern or character and so on. Now either give out real estate information on several homes to half of the students who are estate agents, or let students prepare descriptions of their ideal home for homework. Once you have your dream home specifications, either because you have prepared them or the students have done so for homework, split the class into estate agents and home buyers. Home buyers have a few minutes to interview three or four estate agents and choose a property from those on offer. Estate agents only have one or two houses in their portfolio which they are very keen to sell. House buyers may visit several estate agents within a time limit of a few minutes with each one before making their choice. See which estate agents make the most sales.

This game is adaptable to many topics. Here are a few examples:

Favorite holiday destination: Travel agents and customers
Best product: Salesmen and customers
Favorite day out: Tour guides and customers
Food for the school canteen: Nutritionists and parents
Which school for your child? Headmasters and parents
Which job? Employers and Employees
Which bank? Bank managers and customers (ideal for business English) Give the bank managers the task of choosing a bank and reading up on the terms for homework.
Which party? Hosts describe what their party will be like and guests decide which party they want to go to
Which political party? Party leaders describe their policies and voters decide who to vote for. Allow for some outrageous parties such as the Monster Raving Loony Party from the UK. Be sure students

know they can take on a role rather than express personal views. Have students each prepare a party manifesto for homework that can be used in the pair-work in class.

Which pet? A pet lover tries to sell his idea of the best pet to a potential pet buyer.

Which country? Ambassadors try to attract immigrants to their country. If you have refugees or feel that this is too sensitive for your class play then play the game using imaginary countries that have fantasy ideas such as free food for children and so on.

After you have done it once it will be an extra string to your bow and something you can use over and over again to make your lessons more passionate.

Some help with Grammar

Parts of Speech

Nouns.
Nouns are words that name people, places, things, or ideas.
Before you look at the list of nouns, it is important to note that nouns will fit into more than one category.

For example, the word *train* is a **common noun**, **concrete**, is a **countable**, **singular** noun.

Common Nouns name people, places or things that are not specific.
 man, mountain, state, ocean, country, building, cat, airline, etc.

Proper Nouns name specific people, places, or things.
Walt Disney, Mount Kilimanjaro, Minnesota, Atlantic Ocean, Australia, Empire State

Building, Fluffy, Sun Country, etc.

Abstract Nouns name nouns that you can't perceive with your five senses.
love, wealth, happiness, pride, fear, religion, belief, history, communication, etc.

Concrete Nouns name nouns that you can perceive with your five senses.
house, ocean, Uncle Mike, bird, photograph, banana, eyes, light, sun, dog, suitcase, flowers, etc.

Countable Nouns name nouns that you can count.
bed, cat, movie, train, country, book, phone, match, speaker, clock, pen, David, violin, etc.

Uncountable Nouns name nouns that you can't count.
milk, rice, snow, rain, water, food, music, etc.

Compound Nouns are made up of two or more words.
tablecloth, eyeglasses, New York, photograph, daughter-in-law, pigtails, sunlight,

snowflake, etc.
<u>Collective Nouns</u> refer to things or people as a unit.
bunch, audience, flock, team, group, family, band, village, etc.

Pronouns.

Personal Pronouns.	Singular	Plural

take the place of common and proper nouns.

First Person:
the person or people speaking or writing.

	Singular	Plural
	I	we
	me	us

Second Person:
the person or people being spoken or written to

	you	you

Third Person:
the person, people, or things being spoken or written about.

	Singular	Plural
	she, her	they
	he, him	them
	it	

Relative Pronouns:
relate a subordinate clause to the rest of the sentence

that, which, who,whom, whose, whichever, whoever, whomever

Demonstrative Pronouns:

	Singular	Plural
Represent a thing or things.		
Refers to things that are nearby	This	These
Refers to things that are far away.	That	Those

<u>Indefinite Pronouns:</u>
Refer to something that is unspecified

Singular. anybody, anyone, anything, each, either, everybody, everyone, everything, neither, nobody, no one, nothing, one, somebody, someone, something.

Plural both, few, many, several

Singular or Plural all, any, most, none, some.

Reflexive Pronouns:

End in *self* or *selves*	Singular	Plural

First Person: **the person**
  or **people speaking or writing** Myself Ourselves

Second Person: **the person
or people being spoken to
or written to**   Yourself   Yourselves

Third Person: **the person,
people, or things being
spoken to or written about**   himself,
                                          herself,
                                          itself.   Themselves.

Interrogative Pronouns
are used to ask questions.   what, who, which, whom, whose

Possessive Pronouns
 used to show ownership.   Singular   Plural

Used Before Nouns   my   our
                                          your   your
                                          his, her, its   their

Used Alone   mine   ours
                                          yours   yours
                                          his, hers   theirs

Subject and Object Pronouns
 are used as either the subject or the object in a sentence.   **Singular**   **Plural**

Subject: whom or what the sentence is about   I, you, he   we, you
                                                                    She, he, it.   they.

Object: direct objects, indirect objects,   Me, you, her   Us, you
objects of prepositions.   him, it.   them.

Verbs.

Action verbs.

As their name implies, these verbs show action.

Keep in mind that *action* doesn't always mean *movement*.

Example.
Penelope *thought* about Kangaroos.

In that example, the verb *thought* does not show movement, but it is a mental *action*, and therefore, it is still a verb.

48

There are **many, many action verbs**. Here is random assortment of some action verbs.

Clean, cut, drive, eat, fly, go, live, make, play, tread, run, shower, sweep, smile, shop, sleep, swim, think, throw, trip, walk, wash, work, write, jog, amble, drive, herd, fish, study, read.

Linking Verbs

These types of verbs link the subject of a sentence with a noun or adjective.
Example:
> Lana **became** a famous equestrian.

If you count all of the forms of "to be" as one word, there are 13 linking verbs. Memorize these:

Forms of *be*.   be, am, is, are, was, were, been, being.
Other Linking Verbs.   Appear, become, feel, grow, look, seem, remain, smell, sound, stay, taste, turn.

Helping Verbs

These do just what their name implies. They **help** action verbs or linking verbs. There can be more than one of them used in a single verb phrase.
Example: (used with the action verb *love*)
> **Freda will** love these sausages.

There are only **24 helping verbs**.
Use this chart and memorize them!   Be, am, is, are, was, were, been, being, have,
                                       Have, has, had, could, should, would, may,
                                       Might, must, shall, can, will, do, did, does, having.

Transitive Active
Certain action verbs called *transitive action verbs* transfer action to something called a direct object.

Transitive Passive (A Type of Action Verb)
This type of action verb does not pass any action to anyone or anything.

Subject/Verb

Intransitive Linking Verb
These verbs link the subject to another noun, pronoun, or adjective.

Subject/**linking verb**\predicate noun or adjective

Subject/ **verb**/ direct object

Helping Verb

Helping verbs help the main verb. They are used in sentences with either linking verbs or action verbs.

It's easy to see that they help another verb when you see how they are diagrammed.

Subject/ **helping verb** main verb

Phrasal verb list

Phrasal Verb	**Meaning**	**and then an Example.**

Ask *someone* **out.**   Invite.

John asked Jane out on a date.

Ask around.   Ask many people the same question.

I asked around but nobody was able to help me.

Add up to   *something*. Equal.

All of the answers added up to the same thing.

Back *something* **up**   Reverse.
You will have to back your car up.

Back *someone* **up.**   Support.

My family backed up my decision to quit my job.

Blow up.   Explode.

The truck exploded on impact.

Blow *something* **up.**   Inflate.

The balloons needed to be blown up.

Break down.   Stop working like a machine.

The car broke down in the country.

Break down.   Get upset.

The clerk broke down when she was fired.

Break *something* **down.**   Dismantle.

The machine was broken down to examine the internal parts.

Break in.   To force an entry

Thieves broke into our home.

Break in.   prepare for use.

I had to break in my new shoes.

Break into.   Enter by force.

The Firemen had to break into the burning building.

Break into   Interrupt

The announcer broke into the program with a news flash.

Break up.   End a relationship.

My girl friend and I had to break up when I moved abroad.

Break up.   Start laughing, (informal)

The audience just broke up when the comedian started his act.

Break out.   Escape.

The prisoners broke out of the prison.

Beak out *with something*   Develop a skin condition.

The boy had a terrible rash when he walked through the Poison Ivy.

Bring *someone* **down**   Make sad

This music will bring me down.

Bring *someone* **up**.   Raise a child.

The orphan was brought up in a foster home.

Bring *something* **up**   Raise a subject.

The co-chairman brought up many other options.

Bring *something* **up**.   Vomit

The youngster brought up his entire recent meal.

Call around   Phone many places or people

We called around but could not find the things we needed

Call *someone* **back**   Return a phone call.

I called the company back but the office was closed for the weekend.

Call *something* **off**   Cancel

The groom changed his mind and called the wedding off.

Call on *someone*   Ask for an answer or an opinion.

The teacher called on me to answer the first question.

Call on *someone*.   Visit

We were passing close by so we called on our friends.
Call *someone* **up**   Phone.

We were asked to call up before visiting our neighbors.

Calm down   Relax after being angry

You cannot be rational until you calm down.

Not care.   do not value.

The customer really did not care for the things shown him.

Catch up.   Get alongside another person.

You will have to catch up with him to have a chance of winning.

Catch up.   Get your work load up to date.

I will have to work late to get caught up

Check in.   Register at a hotel or travel terminal.

You have to check in before you can go to your room

Check in.   Report to comply with the specified conditions,.

The parolee had to check in with the Police every week.

Check out.   Leave your hotel.

You have to check out and pay your account when you leave.

Check out.   Look at informally.

You should check out that crazy hairstyle.

Check.   Re-examine.

You need to check that you have the answers correct.

Cheer up   Make happy.

I hope you can relax and cheer up.

Cheer up.   Become happier.

When she received flowers she cheered up.

Chip in.   Everyone helps.

If we all chip in it will not take long to get finished.

Chip in.   Contribute

We can afford that if we all chip in.

Clean up.   Make tidy.

The workers all had to clean up before going home.

Clean up.   To win when gambling.

He was very lucky and cleaned up.

Come across. To find something that was missing.

The search party came across the missing child.

Come across. To change your view-point.

The objector came across and joined the other Council members.

Come apart. Separate.

The house came apart when the Tornado struck

Come down with. Become sick.

The patient came down with a Cold which was severe.

Come forward volunteer to do something.

The witness came forward to give evidence at the trial.

Come from. Originate

The applicant came from a small town.

Count on. Rely.

We need to know if we can count on you.

Cross out. Erase. Draw a line through.

Please cross out the old address on your record sheet.

Cut back. Reduce consumption.

The tenants had to cut back on using water when the supply line was being repaired.

Cut down. Make something fall.

The old tree had to be cut down.

Cut down. Attack verbally.

The prosecutor cut down the hostile witness.

Cut in.   Interrupt.

The cheeky student cut into the teacher's explanation.

Cut in.   To pass closely in front of.

The young driver liked to cut in on the other drivers.

Cut in   Start up a motor or appliance.

The generator will cut in if the mains power goes off line.

Cut off.   To remove.

The tree surgeon cut of the diseased tree limb.

Cut off.   Stop providing.

The electricity was cut of when the bill was not paid.

Cut off.   To swerve in front of.

The car cut off the car he was passing.

Cut off.   To stop payment.

The customer was cut off when he failed to pay his account.

Cut out.   Remove a part by cutting.

The unemployed man cut out the ads for jobs.

Cut out.   Isolate.

The interrupter cut out the lecturer's talk

Cut out.   Disconnect

The electrical system cut out when overloaded.

Do over.   Ransack.

The house was done over by thieves.

Do over.   Repeat.

The work was so bad it had to be done over.

Do away with.   Discard

It is time to do away with those old things.

Do up.   Fasten.

Please do up your coat buttons.

Do up.   Renovate.

The apartment was all done up for re-rental.

Dress up.   Wear nice clothes.

It is advisable to dress up when going to the theater

Drop back.   Go back into a lower position in a group.

The runner dropped back when he became tired.

Drop in/by/over.   Visit.

Drop in whenever you are passing our way.

Drop off.   Help someone get to another place.

The son dropped off his father at the doctor's office.

Drop off.   Disappear.

The fugitive dropped off the world when he escaped.

Drop out.   Quit.

The lazy student dropped out of classes.

Eat out.   Eat at a restaurant.

We usually eat out on Wednesdays.

End up.   Arrive. Eventually. Finally.

We ended up with a movie rental instead of going out.

Fall apart.   Disintegrate.

The dress fell apart in the washing machine.

Fall down.   Drop to the ground.

The picture fell down when the suspending wire broke.

Fall out.   Become free of.

The money fell out of his pocket.

Fall out.   Disagree.

The two friends fell out over an attractive girl

Fall out.   Give up.

The runner fell out of the race.

Fall out.   Become loose or unattached

His hair fell out when he was very young.

Figure out.   Understand. Find the answer.

The engineer figured out the cause of the problem.

Fill in.(Brit. Eng)   Fill in the blank spaces on a form.

You have to fill out the application form.

Fill out.(Am.Eng)   Fill in the blank spaces on a form.

The form must be filled out.

Fill up.   Fill completely.

The man filled up his car's fuel tank.

Find out.   Discover.

You will have to find out the true meaning.

Find out.   Find the answer.

How can we find out where she lives?

Get across/over.   Communicate/ make understandable.

How can we get this information across?

Get along/on.   Relate.

The two got along well.

Get around.   Be mobile.

They rented a car to get around on their holiday.

Get away.   Escape.

The prisoner got away.

Get away.   Evade detection.

The secretary got away with divulging secret information.

Get back.   Return.

We got back from our holiday last week.

Get back.   Retrieve.

We got our notes back from the garbage can.

Get back at.   Get revenge.

The girl got back at her cheating boy friend.

Get back into.   Re-enter.

The retiree got back into exercising regularly.

Get on.   Step in to a vehicle.

The passengers get on to the bus.

Get Over.   Recover from something.

John managed to get over the Flu quickly.

Get over.   Overcome a problem.

The company is in trouble if it cannot get over this crisis.

Get around.   Be mobile.

Even handicapped people get around quite well nowadays.

Get around to.   Finally start to do something that is needed.

Peter finally got around to starting his school project.

Get together.   Join up with.

We can get together on Friday evening if you would like to do so.

Get up.   Get out of bed.

You have to get up early tomorrow.

Get up.   Stand up.

Young people should get up for the elderly.

Get up.   An unusual style of dress.

You look really odd in that get up.

Give away.   Reveal hidden information.

The student gave the cheater away when the teacher asked.

Give away.   Present for marriage.

The father gives the Bride away at the wedding.

Give away.   Reveal by accident.

My sister gave away my secrets.

Give away.   Give a gift.

The lottery winner gave away lots of money.

Give back.   Return something.

Please give this back when you are finished with it.

Give in.   Concede.

The struggling Wrestler gave in to his opponent.

Give out.   Give things to many people.

The lucky boy gave out most of his free candy.

Give out.   Fail.

The support gave out and the wall collapsed.

Give up.   Quit a habit.

The heavy smoker finally gave up his habit.

Give up.   Quit trying.

The course was so difficult I finally gave up

Go after.   To follow.

The detective had to go after the thief.

Go after.   Try to achieve something.

The contestants decided to go after the prizes.

Go against.   Oppose. Compete with.

We are going against the league leaders tomorrow.

Go ahead.   Start, proceed.

Please start eating before the food gets cold.

Go ahead.   Pass in front of.

Please go ahead and go to the head of the line up.

Go back.   Return to where you were.

You must go back to the beginning.

Go out.   Leave home to attend a social event.

We are going out to the theater this evening.

Going out.   Dating.

Charles is going out with Jane now.

Go over.   Review.

The team had to go over the new plans.

Go over. Visit.

We will go over to Peter's house tonight.

Go without.   Suffer lack or deprivation.

If you do not behave you will go without supper.

Grow apart.   Suffer a growing detachment in a relationship.

The couple were growing apart.

Grow back.   Re-grow.

The short hair grew back quickly.

Grow up.   Mature.

The children seem to grow up really quickly.

Grow out of.   Get too big for.

Young Charles is growing out of his clothes quickly.

Grow into.   Grow big enough to fit

The younger brother grew into his elder brother's clothes.

Hand down.   Pass on to another.

My brother handed down his tight clothes to me.

Hand in.   Submit.

We had to hand in our essays as soon as possible.

Hand out.   Distribute.

Will you please hand out these texts to the class.

Hand over.   Give when ordered to do so.

The police insisted that the witness handed over the things he'd found.

Hang in.   Stay positive and hopeful.

If you just hang in there you will succeed.

Hang on.   Wait a short while.

Please hang on while I get my things.

Hang out.   Spend time relaxing.

We usually hang out on Wednesday evenings.

Hang up.   End a phone call.

When you have finished talking please hang up.

Hold back.   Restrain.

The Police have to hold back the crowds.

Hold back.   Hide an emotion.

The jilted girl held back her tears.

Hold on.   Wait a short time.

Please hold on while I transfer this call.

Hold onto.   Keep hold of.

Hold onto your hat when it is windy.

Hold up.   Support.

The gantry holds up the Crane.

Hold up.   Rob.

The bank was robbed by the hold up artists.

Keep on.   Continue.

When you exercise you must keep on doing it.

Keep on.   Retain.

The firm will keep you on if you take courses.

Keep from.   Hide.

We kept our relationship from the other employees.

Keep out.   Stop from entering.

The security people will keep out casual visitors.

Keep up.   Continue at the same rate.

If you come running with us you will have to keep up.

Knock up. Eng.   Wake up

I have to work early tomorrow, please knock me up.

Knock up. American.   Impregnate.

John knocked his girl friend up.

Let down.   Disappoint.

The team was let down by the poor player.

Let down.   Control the descent,

The load was let down slowly.

Let in.   Allow to enter.

The visitors were let in by the Butler.

Look after.   Take care of.

The home help is there to look after the old lady.

Look down on.   Consider inferior.

The boss might look down on his laborers

Look for.   Try to find.

We will have to go out and look for our lost cat.

Look forward to.   Be excited about the future.

The children all look forward to Christmas.

Look into.   Investigate.

The accountant will look into any financial discrepancies.

Look out.   Be careful, vigilant.

Look out, it is dangerous here.

Look out.   Be especially vigilant.

Look out when you walk there we have snakes in the long grass

Look over. Examine.

Will you please look over my work to check for any mistakes.

Look up. Research.

We often have to look up new information.

Look up to. Respect.

The congregation looked up to their new Minister.

Make up. Invent. Lie about.

When asked about his actions the boy made up a good story.

Make up. Enhance one's face.

The actress wore a lot of make up.

Make up. Resolve a difference.

The two friends made up their differences and were very happy.

Mix up. Confuse

The papers were all mixed up and impossible to understand.

Pass away. Die.

The sick man passed away yesterday evening.

Pass out. Faint.

If you are short of breath you may pass out.

Pass out. Give the same thing to many people.

The class monitors passed out the term papers.

Pass up. Do without.

I passed up the job because it was too far to travel.

Pay back.   Return borrowed items.

My neighbor paid back the loan I gave him.

Pay back.   Return an action.

The thieves were paid back by serving a long sentence.

Pay for.   Suffer the consequences.

The boy paid for his earlier bad behavior

Pick out.   Select.

You will have to pick out the things you like.

Point out.   Indicate.

Point out the offender if you see him in the line up.

Put down.   Place something on the table or floor,.

You have to put down what you are holding when you are examined.

Put down.   Disgraced. Offended.

The secretary suffered a huge put down by her new boss.

Put off.   Delay.

The game **was put off because of rain.**

Put out.   Extinguish.

Put out the lights when you leave.

Put out.   Offended.

The stood up date was really put out.

Put together.   Assembled.

The collection was put together by the helpers.

Put up with.   Tolerate.

The problem is we have to tolerate the noise in here.

Put on.   Don clothing.

Please put on your Pajamas.

Put on.   Taken advantage of.

The junior staffers were put on by their co workers.

Run into.   Collided with.

The car ran into the bus at the junction.

Run into.   Meet by accident.

I ran into your brother today.

Run over.   Drive a vehicle over a person or thing.

The car ran over the stray dog.

Run over or through.   Rehears or review.

Please run over your lines before we begin the rehearsal.

Run away.   Leave. Escape.

The truants have run away.

Run out.   Use all up.

We have run out of shampoo.

Run out.   Leave without notice.

The office junior run out when he was accused of stealing.

Send back.   Return.

The horrible meal was sent back to the chef.

Set up.   Arrange, organize.

The display was all set up to view.

Set up.   Trick.

The situation was a set up.

Shop around.   Compare prices.

If you want a bargain you have to shop around.

Show off.   Act special for people watching.

The small boy was all excited and showing of in front of the visitors.

Show off.   Display proudly.

The new model cars needed to be shown of well.

Sleep over.   Stay overnight, informally.

The girls were having a sleep over.

Sort out.   Organize, resolve a problem.

We need to sort out the confusion here.

Stick to.   Continue to do something.

You have to stick to your original plan.

Switch off.   Stop the energy flow.

Please switch off the radio.

Switch on.   Start the energy flow.

Would you please switch on the light.

Take after.   Resemble

The son takes after his father.

Take after. Chase.

Take after that stolen car.

Take apart. Purposely break into pieces.

The auto wreckers take apart their cars.

Take back Return something.

Will you take back that mower to the man next door?

Take back. R etrieve.

He had to take back his angry words.

Take off. Start to fly.

The airplanes take off from an airfield.

Take off. Leave spontaneously.

The angry secretary just took off after the argument.

Take off. Remove some clothing.

Please take off your damp overcoat.

Take out. Take home, prepared food.

I'm too tired to cook can we get take out?

Take out. Remove something.

The Dentist may have to take out a tooth.

Take out. Date.

My brother wants to take out the girl next door.

Tear up. Rip apart.

You need to tear up the old pages.

Think back.   Recall.

You may have to think back and remember.

Think over.   Consider.

You need to think over what you intend to say.

Throw away.   Dispose of.

The worn out parts need to be thrown away.

Turn down.   Refuse or reject.

Are you going to turn down my offer?

Turn down.   Reduce the volume.

Please turn down the noisy radio.

Turn off.   Stop the flow

Can you please turn off that dripping tap?

Turn off.   Discourage.

You may find the pictures are a turn off.

Turn on.   Start the flow.

Please turn on the hot water.

Turn on.   Get interested.

The low cut dress was quite a turn on.

Turn up.   Increase the volume.

Please turn up the radio.

Turn up.   Arrive unexpectedly.

Can we just turn up at your parent's house.

Try on.   Sample clothing.

Try on this dress to see if it fits.

Try on.   Try to cheat.

The salesman was just trying on when he offered the goods.

Try out.   Test.

You should try out those new shoes.

Use up.   Finish the supply.

We must use up what we have before we re-order.

Wake up   arouse a sleeper.

Will you please wake me up at seven O'Clock.

Warm up.   Increase the temperature.

Mother will warm up you late dinner.

Warm up.   Prepare for exercise.

You need to warm up before you run.

Wear off.   Fade away.

The effects of the drugs will wear off soon.

Work out.   Exercise.

I have a daily work out in the Gym.

Work out.   Be successful.

I am sure that things will work out.

Work out.   Make a calculation.

The Professor had to work out the answer,

Adjectives.

Proper Adjectives.

These are formed from **proper nouns**.
They always begin with a **capital letter**.

Proper Noun	Proper Adjective
America	American
Britain	British
Canada	Canadian
China	Chinese
Christianity	Christian
France	French

Articles

There are only **three** of these special types of adjectives: **a**, **an**, and **the**.

Regular Comparatives and Superlatives

Most adjectives can be described in **degrees**. This means that something can have more or less of the adjective's quality.

Regular comparatives end in—*er* or start with ***more***.

Regular superlatives end in—*est* or start with ***most***.

Positive	Comparative	Superlative
Ambitious	More ambitious	Most ambitious
Cold	Colder	Coldest
Comfortable	More comfortable	Most comfortable
Dry	Drier	Driest
Enchanting	More enchanting	Most enchanting
Funny	Funnier	Funniest
Hot	Hotter	Hottest

Organized	More organized	Most organized
Pretty	Prettier	Prettiest
Radiant	More radiant	Most radiant
Sharp	Sharper	Sharpest
Wavy	Wavier	Waviest

Irregular Comparatives and Superlatives

These can still be given in degrees, but they don't follow the patterns listed above.

Positive	**Comparative**	**Superlative**
Bad	Worse	Worst
Good	Better	Best
Little	Less	Least
Many	More	Most

Adjectives That Cannot Be Comparative or Superlative

Some adjectives **don't have degrees**. There is only one level of these adjectives. (For example, something cannot be **more half** than something else. It either **is** half, or it **isn't**.)

Entire, fatal, final, half, main, pregnant.

Adverbs.
Adverbs are words that describe—or modify—verbs, adjectives, and other adverbs.

They tell us *how, when, where, to what extent,* and *why.*

Adverbs that tell us How?

A: absentmindedly, adoringly, awkwardly
B: beautifully, briskly, brutally
C: carefully, cheerfully, competitively
E: eagerly, effortlessly, extravagantly
G: girlishly, gracefully, grimly
L: lazily, lifelessly, loyally
Q: quietly, quickly, quizzically

R: really, recklessly, remorsefully, ruthlessly
S: savagely, sloppily, so, stylishly
U: unabashedly, unevenly, urgently
W: well, wishfully, worriedly

Adverbs that tell us *When?*

A: after, afterwards, annually
B: before
D: daily
N: never, now
S: soon, still
T: then, today, tomorrow
W: weekly, when
Y: yesterday

Adverbs that tell us *Where?*

A: abroad, anywhere, away
E: everywhere
H: here, home
I: in, inside
O: out, outside
S: somewhere
T: there
U: underground, upstairs

Adverbs that tell us t*o what extent?*

E: extremely
N: not (this includes *n't*)
Q: quite
R: rather, really
T: terribly, too
V: very

Comparative and Superlative Adverbs

Positive	Comparative	Superlative

Badly	Worse	Worst
Carefully	More carefully	Most carefully
Little	Less	Least
Much	More	Most
Soon	Sooner	Soonest
Well	Better	Best

Prepositions

A   aboard, about, above, across, after, against, ahead of, along, amid,

amidst, among, around, as, as far as, as of, aside from, at, athwart, atop

B   barring, because of, before, behind, below, beneath, beside, besides,

between, beyond, but, by, by means of

C   circa, concerning

D   despite, down, during

E   except, except for, excluding

F

far from, following, for, from

I

in place of, in spite of, including, inside, instead of, into in, in accordance with, in addition to, in case of, in front of, in lieu of,

L   like

M   minus

N   near, next to

O   of, off, on, on account of, on behalf of, on top of, onto, opposite, out, out of, outside, over

P   past, plus, prior to

R   regarding, regardless of

S

    save, since

T

    than, through, till, to, toward, towards

U

    under, underneath, unlike, until, up, upon

V

    versus, via

W

    with, with regard to, within, without

Seeing a list of prepositions is great, but you also need to understand what prepositions are.

Remember that prepositions are words that show the relationship between a noun or a pronoun and some other word in the sentence.

They are ALWAYS found in prepositional phrases.

Prepositional phrases are groups of words that act as a single part of speech, so all of the words act together as either an adjective or an adverb.

They always start with a preposition and end with a noun or pronoun.

Here are some examples of prepositional phrases: at the movie. up the tree. around the block.

Conjunctions.

Conjunctions are words that join two or more words, phrases, or clauses

Coordinating Conjunctions

There are only seven of these.

Here they are:

    for, and, nor, but, or, yet, so

You can remember them using the acronym **FANBOYS.**

Subordinating Conjunctions

There are many subordinating conjunctions. This list does not include all of them.

Example: I will eat broccoli **after** I eat this cookie.

A: after, although, as, as if, as long as, as much as, as soon as, as though

B: because, before, by the time

E: even if, even though

I: if, in order that, in case

L: lest

O: once, only if

P: provided that

S: since, so that

T: than, that, though, till

U: unless, until

W: when, whenever, where, wherever, while

Correlative Conjunctions

These are always used in pairs.

Example: This cookie contains **neither** chocolate **nor** nuts.

both   and
either   or
neither   nor
not only   but also
whether   or

Insert #12. Interjections.

Interjections are words that show emotion. They are not grammatically related to the rest of the sentence.

A:	aha, ahem, ahh, ahoy, alas, arg, aw
B:	bam, bingo, blah, boo, bravo, brrr
C:	cheers, congratulations
D:	dang, drat, darn, duh
E:	eek, eh, encore, eureka
F:	fiddlesticks
G:	gadzooks, gee, gee whiz, golly, goodbye, goodness, good grief, gosh
H:	ha-ha, hallelujah, hello, hey, hmm, holy buckets, holy cow, holy smokes, hot dog, huh?, humph, hurray
O:	oh, oh dear, oh my, oh well, ooops, ouch, ow
P:	phew, phooey, pooh, pow
R:	rats
S:	shh, shoo
T:	thanks, there, tut-tut
U:	uh-huh, uh-oh, ugh
W:	wahoo, well, whoa, whoops, wow
Y:	yeah, yes, yikes, yippee, yo, yuck

The seven aspects of learning

Learning is made easier for the students and what is learned is remembered longer when the following factors are used.

READINESS—Ensure students are mentally, physically and emotionally ready to learn.
To learn, a person must be ready to do so. An effective teacher understands this necessity and does the utmost to provide well conceived motivation. If a student has a strong purpose, a clear objective and a sound reason for learning something, progress will be much better than if motivation were lacking. It is recommended that the lessons be started with an attention getting opening and the students are told what they will be learning and why it is important for them to have the information the will get and where it fits into the overall picture.

It is advisable to plan for reviews of the lesson material. Students start to forget the moment they leave the instructional environment. The greatest rate of forgetting occurs during the first *24-48 hours* after learning the material. Ohio State University has carried out extensive research in this area and has designed a recommended schedule of when reviews should be done.

The graph curve of forgetting is very steep initially — within two days students will remember less than 70% of what they learned. At the end of the month without reviews students will only remember approximately 40% of lesson material.

PRIMACY—Present new knowledge or skills correctly the first time. (Teach it right the first time.) When students are presented with new knowledge or skills, the first impression received is almost unshakeable. This means that what you teach must be correct the first time. Students may forget the details of lessons, but will retain an overall image of the knowledge for a long time. I think you will agree that if you ask someone to forget something and remember something different. They will remember what they were asked to forget.

To maintain at least a 70% level, a review should be conducted within two days.

After learning material a second time the curve flattens out somewhat, but after seven days the student is back down to the 70% level.

Another review and the curve really flattens. The student will be above 70% retention until approximately day 28.

A review at this time will generally cause long lasting retention of lesson material. The amount of time required for reviews reduces each time a review is conducted.

Initial lesson:	fifty minutes.
First review:	fifteen minutes.
Second review:	Ten minutes.

RELATIONSHIP—Present lessons in the logical sequence of known to unknown, simple to complex, easy to difficult.

This particular learning factor emphasizes the necessity for your student to understand relationships between new and old facts, or between ideas and skills if learning is to take place.

Present lessons in a logical sequence:

1. known to unknown;
2. easy to difficult;
3. concrete to abstract;
4. simple to complex;
5. familiar to unfamiliar.

Present new material in stages, confirming that students have mastered one stage before proceeding to the next. The length of time for each stage would depend on the complexity of the material covered.

Reinforce students' learning of new facts or ideas by frequently summarizing the major points of your lesson.

Use examples and comparisons to show how the new material being learned is really not much different from that already known by your students. The examples you use may be real or imaginary as the main purpose of an example is to paint a verbal picture so students can visualize relationships between the new material and things that have happened before. This is called using verbal aids for your instruction

EXERCISE—Keep the students engaged in meaningful activity.
Meaningful mental or physical activity is essential if learning is to occur.
If students are able to answer questions involving the words "how" and "why", it usually means that they have a good understanding of the subject.

INTENSITY—Use dramatic, realistic or unexpected things, as they are long remembered.
Students learn more from dramatic or exciting experiences than from boring ones.
The Learning Factor of Intensity implies that students will learn more from real experiences than from substitutes. You will have to use your imagination to develop vivid experiences for dramatic or realistic effects.

Show enthusiasm and sincerity for the subject you are teaching.

Attempt to employ a wide range of speech variation in rate, volume and pitch to keep students attentive.

Use appropriate and effective gestures while explaining major points. The lesson will seem to "come alive" and the points made will make a greater impression on your student.
Use a variety of training aids to appeal to as many senses as possible. Each aid must relate directly to the subject matter being taught.

EFFECT—Ensure students gain a feeling of satisfaction from having taken part in a lesson.

Learning is strengthened when accompanied by a pleasant or satisfying feeling. Students will learn and remember more under these conditions than when feelings of defeat, frustration, anger or futility are developed.

> Whatever the learning situation, it should contain elements that affect your student positively and give feelings of satisfaction. Each learning experience does not have to be entirely successful, nor do students have to master each lesson completely; however, a student's chance of success will be increased with a sense of accomplishment and a pleasant learning experience.

Involve students in the lesson by developing some of the new material from them. This can be done by asking students questions related to the subject and allowing student contributions of knowledge and ideas

Throughout your lessons, obtain feedback from students by asking questions, observing the performance of a skill and watching for facial expressions that show a lack of understanding. You must respond to any feedback by answering questions and providing assistance and correction where needed.

Show students how to improve and offer praise when improvement occurs.

Back up all your statements with reasons. Whenever you tell students something give the reason behind it. For example, you say to a student,

Avoid ridicule or sarcasm. You may feel that it might take the place of humor; however, students seldom have the same feeling, especially if they are the butt of the remark.

Arrange each lesson so that when a student does something correctly, there is a reward. This reward can be in the form of sincere, honest praise.

RECENCY—Summarize and practice the important points at the end of each lesson, as last things learned and practiced will be remembered longest.

> Other things being equal, the last things learned are best remembered. Conversely, the longer students are removed from a new fact or even an understanding, the more difficulty they will have remembering it. The need for a reviews was stated earlier when a full cycle has been completed — review — learn new material — review, etc.

Ensure that students receive a thorough summary of the important points towards the end of each lesson.

After each sequence within an exercise or class presentation, ask questions on the material or summarize the "need-to know" material.

Conduct a test as the final part of your lesson.

At intervals throughout the course, conduct review periods in which no new material is taught, but reinforcement is obtained.

> Attempt to finish lessons with practice of the most important parts of the lesson. This applies to solo lessons as well as dual exercises. Remember, students practice knowledge by answering questions and they practice skills by doing.

Hints on Classroom management

The title for this part may seem out of place but if you consider the true meaning of the words you will realize that like in business the term does apply. The lessons in the classroom regardless of the number of students do need planning, organization, giving instructions, analyzing responses as well as thinking ahead. If we think about these terms we come to appreciate how they help the teacher. The teacher does need to plan for the time needed for each lesson as well as the homework assignments that will be needed.

Consideration has also has to be given for the possibility of the use of supplementary materials.

Organization.

Organization and planning are closely related. Before you start your lessons you have to organize your materials as well as the use of your own and the student's use of time. Your lesson plans should reflect this so you can stay n track during the classes.

Giving instructions.

Many teachers can remember the times when things did not go right because the instructions were badly given. Students rapidly lose interest when they cannot understand what is expected of them. Think carefully when planning the lesson activities and materials to be used.

Analyzing responses.

Teachers need to give instructions but they also must be able to analyze the responses. Written work is easy to analyze but the oral responses can present difficulties at time. It may be noisy and so it is not easy to hear what is said. The situation is often aggravated by the pronunciation problems of the student and the monotone they often use.

It is advisable to be cautious when correcting the mistakes of the students. Many students do not like to be constantly corrected and are very sensitive to this kind of treatment.

It is far better to let the students make their mistakes and then correct the ones that they do not catch themselves a little later on. Correct the mistakes in private and avoid correcting more than the main three mistakes at any one time if you correct too many the student may feel discouraged and quit.

Think ahead.

Good teachers are flexible. They are aware of what they want to achieve, but they also know how and when to discard a lesson plan and respond to the specific needs of the students in the class or to respond to an unexpected piece of language production.

As a teacher you need to keep your lesson plan and your specific aims in mind. Your can then mentally monitor what is actually happening in the class.

Realistic aims and objectives.

If you have thought carefully about your planning and organization you will know what your want the class to achieve. As a good teacher you will know what each individual is capable of achieving. You have to remember that what is good for one student is not necessarily good for another.

You need to be able to encourage the slower students and set more ambitious targets for the better ones.

Success is relative to the student's ability.

You also need realistic aims and objectives for yourself. You need to be able to plan your own development as a teacher and progress over time.

Summation.

We have now reached the end of this short guide and hope that you found it interesting and usefull.

There is lots of information available on the internet that can expand on what has been presented here. It is highly reccommend that you read the websites listed on the next page. These are very informative.

It is hoped you continue with your search for things that help you in your chosen career and become a very good teacher for your students.

the things herein are things that have been learned while teaching and many of them were not available, either in courses or books at that time.

What more can be said other than good luck in your future.

Sincerely.

John D. Trubon.

Some useful Websites

http://www.edge.org/3rd_culture/boroditsky09/boroditsky09_index.html
http://www.englishpage.com/irregularverbs/irregularverbs.html
http://www.languageinstinct.blogspot.com/2006/10/stress-timed-rhythm-of-english.html

http://www.kidshealth.org/teen/your_mind/emotions/culture_shock.html

http://www.englishclub.com/grammar/
http://www.eslkidstuff.com/gamesmenu.htm
http://esl-activities-children.html
http://www.teachchildrenesl.com

http://www.teachingenglishgames.com/3-5.htm
http://www.teachingenglishgames.com/games/allchange.htm
http://www.teachingenglishgames.com/Articles/Learning_Styles.htm
http://www.teachingenglishgames.com/adults.htm
http://www.mes-english.com/games.php

http://www.bogglesworldesl.com/
http://www.englishclub.com/

http://www.esincanada.com

http://www.lifehack.org/articles/lifehack/fifty-50-tools-which-can-help-you-in—writing.html